Divine Mercy Minutes with Jesus

Divine Mercy Minutes with Jesus

Praying Daily on Jesus' Words from the *Diary of St. Faustina*

Arranged and Introduced by
Rev. George W. Kosicki, CSB

2015

Available from:
Marian Helpers Center
Stockbridge, MA 01263

Imprimi Potest:
Very Rev. Daniel Cambra, MIC
Provincial Superior
June 29, 2008

Library of Congress Catalog Number: 2008921625

ISBN: 978-1-59614-193-3

Editing and Proofreading: David Came and Mary Flannery

Cover and Page Design: Kathy Szpak

Cover and interior image: www.us.fotolia.com

For texts from the English Edition of *Diary of St. Maria Faustina Kowalska*

Nihil Obstat:
George H. Pearce, SM
Former Archbishop of Suva, Fiji

Imprimatur:
Joseph F. Maguire
Bishop of Springfield, MA
April 9, 1984

Printed in the United States of America

Dedication

To St. Maria Faustina of the Most Blessed Sacrament and St. John Paul II, the Great Mercy Pope.

Acknowledgements

Thanks to Fr. Jack Fabian, who first challenged me to work on this book; to David Came, executive editor of Marian Press, who from the first sharing of the idea gave the title *Divine Mercy Minutes with Jesus* and then encouraged me with the idea of a prayer response to the words of Jesus; to Betty and Mike Clemens, who started me off on the collection by producing a xerox copy of the latest printing of St. Faustina's *Diary* (2006), so that I could mark and cut and paste the words of Jesus for the 30 themes; for Chuck Roelant, who, with his mathematical mind, solved the puzzle of organizing the 366 days of entries; for Pat Menatti, who so bravely typed my handwritten text; to the continuous intercession of my "Mercy Team" Mary, the Mother of Mercy, St. Faustina, and the St. Pope John Paul II.

Introduction

The words of Jesus in this collection of daily readings from the *Diary of Saint Maria Faustina Kowalska* are those He addressed both to her and to us. They focus on our spiritual life and our world mission of living and spreading the message of Divine Mercy. To help focus our prayer on Jesus' words, I composed a personal prayer response for each day.

As I consider the words of Jesus to St. Faustina, I am amazed at the last written words of Pope John Paul II, proclaimed the day after his death (April 3, 2005). They summarize his personal spiritual life and his prayer of mercy for the whole world. He quotes Jesus' words from the *Diary*:

> **Jesus, I trust in You!** (*Diary*, 47).
>
> **Have mercy on us and on the whole world** (*Diary*, 476).

Many words of Jesus recorded in the *Diary* on The Divine Mercy message and devotion have been proclaimed. But there are still many treasures of Jesus that need to be mined by reflection and prayer. I especially stress *the global consciousness* of the words of Jesus in these daily readings and then in my personal prayer responses. Our life and mission is to be a *presence* of God's mercy in the world and to proclaim God's mercy to a world desperately in need of healing.

May these daily words of Jesus be a spark that enkindles "the fire of mercy" to be "witnesses of mercy to the world" (John Paul II, August 17, 2002, on the occasion of consecrating the Basilica of The Divine Mercy in Krakow, Poland, and entrusting the whole world to The Divine Mercy). May these words of Jesus encourage and challenge us to "trust in Jesus even more" in preparation for His final coming!

This gathering of daily words of Jesus was inspired by *Divine Mercy Minutes: Daily Gems of St. Faustina to Transform Your Prayer Life* (published 2006). That first daily devotional focused on the words of St. Faustina, while this one focuses on Jesus' words. Each thematic topic is introduced by an explanation and exhortation as in *Divine Mercy Minutes*. As mentioned earlier, in this collection, I reflect on each of the entries of the words of Jesus with a personal prayer. My hope is that these prayers may help us more effectively absorb the words of Jesus and encourage us to respond to them ourselves.

Further, this devotional follows the convention of the *Diary* for boldface. That is, the words of Jesus are in boldface. Please note as well that an index to themes is provided in the back of this book, so you can study particular themes at any time.

The words of saintly visionaries, like St. Faustina in her *Diary,* are private revelations of the prophets of our time; they are prophetic revelations. They apply Sacred Scripture and Sacred Tradition to our present world so much in need of Divine Mercy. I find it significant that saintly prophets are listed by St. Paul immediately after the Apostles (see Eph 2:20; Eph 4:12; 1 Cor 13:28).

Who are the prophets of our time if not the saintly visionaries? The world more than ever needs to hear and obey the prophetic words of the visionaries of our time, calling us to turn with trust to the mercy of God, *now* while it is still time for mercy!

Making these bold statements about saintly visionaries and prophets of our time, such as St. Faustina, should be balanced by the knowledge that their messages remain private revelations. So, in the case of the words of Jesus to St. Faustina, the reader should be mindful that they do not carry the weight of Public Revelation like the words of Jesus in the Gospels themselves.

Public Revelation, especially Scripture as the seminal deposit of the faith, is the touchstone in considering private revelation. Thus, the revelations of the Merciful Savior to St. Faustina must always be considered in light of Jesus Christ as presented in the Gospels and the mercy of God in Scripture as a whole. In fact, this was the disposition of mind and heart of St. Faustina as a faithful daughter of the Church.

With all this in mind, may *Divine Mercy Minutes with Jesus* help you grow daily in your personal relationship with the Merciful Savior. May you unite yourself to His merciful Heart, as did St. Faustina, and grow in deeper trust in Him.

Trust/Distrust

January 1 – 14

Jesus told St. Faustina, **The graces of My mercy are drawn by means of one vessel only, and that is — trust** (*Diary*, 1578). Growing in trust is key to developing a deep and abiding relationship with the Lord Jesus. The more we trust in the Lord the more graces we receive from Him, and He rejoices in giving them to us.

On the other hand, when we distrust Jesus, He is hurt because we have refused His mercy. We wound His merciful Heart, since He loves us and wants to pour out His mercy upon us. Yet He so respects our human freedom, which He created, that He will not violate it by forcing His mercy on us.

In our relationship with Jesus, trust is our faith, hope, and love in action. Trust is an action verb that takes in all three. It combines the past focus of our faith in what Jesus did, the present "now" dimension of His love for us, and the future dimension of hope because of what He has prepared for us in heaven.

Trust, then, means to believe in Jesus, to love Him, and to hope in Him. It means to be totally absorbed in Jesus as our Lord and Savior, to reply completely on Him. We desire to have His thoughts, His will, His power, His Heart, and His total trust in the Father.

Now, why is trust in Jesus so important? Because it is our response to God's great mercy. In fact, "Jesus, I trust in You!" is the summary statement of The Divine Mercy message and devotion that the Savior gave to St. Faustina. That is why the Lord Jesus asked that we personally sign the image of The Divine Mercy with the words "Jesus, I trust in You!" Our very praying "Jesus, I trust in You!" is an act of trust — an act of faith, hope, and love in Him. It can and should express the deepest desire of our heart.

May the powerful words of Jesus on trust encourage you to pray frequently and earnestly: "Jesus, I trust in You!"

The Role of Priests

I desire that priests proclaim this great mercy of Mine towards souls of sinners. Let the sinner not be afraid to approach Me. The flames of mercy are burning Me — clamoring to be spent; I want to pour them out upon these souls (*Diary,* 50).

My Prayer Response

Jesus, inspire priests to proclaim to sinners Your mercy. May the flames of mercy that burn You, burn out the sins of those who receive Your mercy.

Distrust Is Tearing at My Insides

Jesus complained to me in these words, **Distrust on the part of souls is tearing at My insides. The distrust of a chosen soul causes Me even greater pain; despite My inexhaustible love for them they do not trust Me. Even My death is not enough for them. Woe to the soul that abuses these** [gifts] (*Diary*, 50).

My Prayer Response:

Jesus, open the hearts of distrusting souls, especially the hearts of chosen souls to Your mercy. As they receive Your mercy, may they give You joy!

Hurt by a Soul's Distrust

Oh, how much I am hurt by a soul's distrust! Such a soul professes that I am Holy and Just, but does not believe that I am Mercy and does not trust in My Goodness. Even the devils glorify My Justice but do not believe in My Goodness.

My Heart rejoices in this title of Mercy (*Diary*, 300).

My Prayer Response:

O Jesus, may distrusting souls, by Your special grace, profess and proclaim that You are mercy and goodness Itself! Hear my prayer that Your Heart may rejoice as these souls turn to You with trust.

Believe My Wounds

My Heart is sorrowful, Jesus said, **because even chosen souls do not understand the greatness of My mercy. Their relationship [with Me] is, in certain ways, imbued with mistrust. Oh, how much that wounds My Heart! Remember My Passion, and if you do not believe My words, at least believe My wounds** (*Diary*, 379).

My Prayer Response:

O my Jesus, may my prayer bring joy to Your Heart as You pierce the hearts of even chosen souls who mistrust You in some ways. May they remember Your Passion and believe Your wounds suffered for them.

Love and Mercy Itself

Tell [all people], **My daughter, that I am Love and Mercy itself. When a soul approaches Me with trust, I fill it with such an abundance of graces that it cannot contain them within itself, but radiates them to other souls** (*Diary,* 1074).

My Prayer Response:

Jesus, You are Love and Mercy itself. I trust in You! Fill me with so much grace that it radiates out to others. May I be a channel for Your mercy, a means of grace for others.

The Bowels of My Mercy

Write this: Everything that exists is enclosed in the bowels of My mercy, more deeply than an infant in its mother's womb. How painfully distrust of My goodness wounds Me! Sins of distrust wound Me most painfully (*Diary,* 1076).

My Prayer Response:

Jesus, how deeply and tenderly You love us. Help me to trust in You even more! May my trust in You bring You consolation in the painful wounds You suffer because of sins of distrust.

Mercy for Tormented Souls

[Let] the greatest sinners place their trust in My mercy. They have the right before others to trust in the abyss of My mercy. My daughter, write about My mercy towards tormented souls (*Diary,* 1146).

My Prayer Response:

Jesus, may tormented and hardened sinners turn with trust to Your mercy. Reveal to them that Your mercy is forgiveness for the seemingly unforgivable sin. May Your mercy bring them peace, joy, and healing.

Appeal to My Mercy

Souls that make an appeal to My mercy delight Me. To such souls I grant even more graces than they ask. I cannot punish even the greatest sinner if he makes an appeal to My compassion, but on the contrary, I justify him in My unfathomable and inscrutable mercy (*Diary*, 1146).

My Prayer Response:

Jesus, I appeal to Your mercy for me a sinner and for mercy on the whole world. Help all of us to appeal to Your great mercy. May we be justified by Your unfathomable and inscrutable mercy!

A Living Fountain of Mercy

Today the Lord said to me, **I have opened My Heart as a living fountain of mercy. Let all souls draw life from it. Let them approach this sea of mercy with great trust. Sinners will attain justification, and the just will be confirmed in good. Whoever places his trust in My mercy will be filled with My divine peace at the hour of death** (*Diary,* 1520).

My Prayer Response:

Lord Jesus, I come to Your open Heart, a living fountain of mercy, an ocean of mercy — with trust in You! I come and appeal to Your mercy both for sinners and for the just that we may all be filled with Your divine peace at the hour of death.

Even Chosen Souls Hurt Me

Jesus complained to me of how painful to Him is the unfaithfulness of chosen souls **and My Heart is even more wounded by their distrust after a fall. It would be less painful if they had not experienced the goodness of My Heart** (*Diary,* 1532).

My Prayer Response:

Jesus, I confess my unfaithfulness and need for deeper trust in You. May I cry out to You in the words of the father interceding for his son possessed by a mute spirit: "I do believe. Help my lack of trust!" (Mk 9:24).

Hearts Open to My Mercy

Tell souls not to place within their own hearts obstacles to My mercy, which so greatly wants to act within them. My mercy works in all those hearts which open their doors to it. Both the sinner and the righteous person have need of My mercy. Conversion, as well as perseverance, is a grace of My mercy (*Diary,* 1577).

My Prayer Response:

Lord Jesus, help me to be more present to Your presence in my heart. I pray for the grace of Your mercy that I may persevere in keeping my heart open to You. And I pray that the hardened hearts of sinners may be softened for conversion, which is also a grace of Your mercy.

Boundless Trust in My Mercy

Let souls who are striving for perfection particularly adore My mercy, because the abundance of graces which I grant them flows from My mercy. I desire that these souls distinguish themselves by boundless trust in My mercy. I Myself will attend to the sanctification of such souls. I will provide them with everything they will need to attain sanctity (*Diary*, 1578).

My Prayer Response:

Lord Jesus, I am striving for perfection, but I really need more of Your mercy. I am nothing without You. Teach me and all souls striving for sanctity how to adore Your mercy and to trust in You still more!

The Vessel of Trust

The graces of My mercy are drawn by means of one vessel only, and that is — trust. Thc more a soul trusts, the more it will receive. Souls that trust boundlessly are a great comfort to Me, because I pour all the treasures of My graces into them (*Diary*, 1578).

My Prayer Response:

Lord Jesus, expand my capacity to trust in You! I and so many souls need and want more of Your mercy. Help us with Your mercy to desire more, to ask for more, so we may receive more graces. Fill our hearts with thanksgiving for Your mercy and help us share the graces we receive.

Ask for Much

I rejoice that [souls] ask for much, because it is My desire to give much, very much. On the other hand, I am sad when souls ask for little, when they narrow their hearts (*Diary,* 1578).

My Prayer Response:

Lord Jesus, I want to please You and have You rejoice as I ask, seek, and knock for more and more of Your mercy not only for myself but for those who "narrow their hearts" and ask for so little. Expand all of our hearts, so we can trust more and receive more.

Beg for Mercy

January 15 – 24

The Lord explains to St. Faustina, the secretary of His mercy, that one of her duties is to beg for His mercy, especially for sinners: **My daughter, secretary of My mercy, your duty is not only to write about and proclaim My mercy, but also to beg for this grace for** [sinners]**, so that they too may glorify My mercy** (*Diary*, 1160). Our need and the whole world's need for mercy is so great that, like St. Faustina, we are to beg for it.

Similarly, in the conclusion of his encyclical *Rich in Mercy (Dives in Misericordia)*, Pope John Paul II begins by emphasizing the Church's right and duty to appeal for God's mercy in light of the evils of our time. He even goes so far as to describe this as a "prayer that is a cry for the mercy of God":

> At no time and in no historical period — especially at a moment as critical as our own — can the Church forget *the prayer that is a cry for the mercy of God* amid the many forms of evil which weigh upon humanity and threaten it. Precisely this is the fundamental right and duty of the Church in Christ Jesus, her right and duty towards God and towards humanity. The more the human conscience succumbs to secularization, loses its sense of the very meaning of the word "mercy," moves away from God and distances itself from the mystery of mercy, the more *the Church has the*

> *right and the duty* to appeal to the God of mercy "with loud cries" (RIM, 15, emphasis in the original text).

Given this encouragement from John Paul II, who was the Great Mercy Pope, let's join St. Faustina in begging for God's mercy by storming heaven for it with our own "loud cries." Let's especially think of sinners and those who are closest to us as we beg for God's mercy. May the words of Jesus that follow inspire us to embrace this task, realizing that, as members of the Church, it is our right and duty.

A Way to Beg

After Communion, I heard the voice saying, **My daughter, look into the abyss of My mercy and give praise and glory to this mercy of Mine. Do it in this way: Gather all sinners from the entire world and immerse them in the abyss of My mercy. I want to give Myself to souls; I yearn for souls, My daughter. On the day of My feast, the Feast of Mercy, you will go through the whole world and bring fainting souls to the spring of My mercy. I shall heal and strengthen them** (*Diary*, 206).

My Prayer Response:

Thank You, Lord Jesus, for teaching us a way to beg for Your mercy on souls. As the Church, we, Your Body, immerse them in the ocean of Your mercy — "baptizing" them in Your mercy. We plunge all fainting souls in the world into the abyss of Your mercy.

The Power of a Confident Soul

On one occasion the Lord said to me, **My daughter, your confidence and love restrain My justice, and I cannot inflict punishment because you hinder Me from doing so.** Oh, how great is the power of a soul filled with confidence! (*Diary*, 198).

My daughter, for the sake of your sincere and generous love, I grant [certain souls who displease Me] **many graces although they are not asking Me for them. But I am doing so because of the promise I have made to you** (*Diary*, 383).

My Prayer Response:

Lord Jesus, I join St. Faustina in her great trust and love of You to restrain Your justice and to call down many graces of Your mercy on this world, which is so in need of mercy. I particularly remember the souls of those I know who are far from You.

For the Whole World

My daughter, I have inclined My Heart to your requests. Your assignment and duty here on earth is to beg for mercy for the whole world. No soul will be justified until it turns with confidence to My mercy, and this is why the first Sunday after Easter is to be the Feast of Mercy. On that day, priests are to tell everyone about My great and unfathomable mercy. I am making you the [dispenser] **of My mercy. Tell the confessor that the Image is to be on view in the church and not within the enclosure in that convent. By means of this Image I shall be granting many graces to souls; so, let every soul have access to it** (*Diary*, 570).

My Prayer Response:

Lord Jesus I unite myself with St. Faustina, the dispenser of Your Mercy, to beg for mercy on the whole world. May every soul have access to the image of You as The Divine Mercy and to the Feast of Mercy.

Beg Mercy for Loved Ones

On one occasion, after a person had asked me for prayer, when I met the Lord I said to Him, "Jesus, I especially love those souls whom You love." And Jesus answered, **And as for Me, I bestow special graces on those souls for whom you intercede** (*Diary*, 599).

After Holy Communion today, I spoke at length to the Lord Jesus about people who are special to me. Then I heard these words: **My daughter, don't be exerting yourself so much with words. Those whom you love in a special way, I too love in a special way, and for your sake, I shower My graces upon them. I am pleased when you tell Me about them, but don't be doing so with such excessive effort** (*Diary*, 739).

My Prayer Response:

Lord Jesus, shower with mercy all the people that we love in a special way as we intercede for them and for the whole world. Lord, I especially remember my family members and close friends.

The Fruit of Begging

On the First Friday of the month, before Communion, I saw a large ciborium filled with sacred hosts. A hand placed the ciborium in front of me, and I took it in my hands. There were a thousand living hosts inside. Then I heard a voice, **These are hosts which have been received by the souls for whom you have obtained the grace of true conversion during this Lent.** That was a week before Good Friday (*Diary*, 640).

Then suddenly I saw the Lord, who clasped me to His Heart and said to me, **My daughter, do not weep, for I cannot bear your tears. I will grant you everything you ask for, but stop crying.** And I was filled with great joy, and my spirit, as usual, was drowned in Him as in its only treasure (*Diary*, 928).

My Prayer Response:

Lord Jesus, thank You for Your loving and tender response to St. Faustina's intercession for souls. It encourages us to be loving and tender in our intercession for souls in need of Your mercy.

Our Duty

December 16, [1936]. I have offered this day for Russia. ... After Holy Communion, Jesus said to me, **I cannot suffer that country any longer. Do not tie my hands, My daughter.** I understood that if it had not been for the prayers of souls that are pleasing to God, that whole nation would have already been reduced to nothingness (*Diary,* 818).

When once I asked the Lord Jesus how He could tolerate so many sins and crimes and not punish them, the Lord answered me, **I have eternity for punishing** [these]**, and so I am prolonging the time of mercy for the sake of** [sinners]**. But woe to them if they do not recognize this time of My visitation. My daughter, secretary of My mercy, your duty is not only to write about and proclaim My mercy, but also to beg for this grace for them, so that they too may glorify My mercy** (*Diary,* 1160).

My Prayer Response:

Lord Jesus, thank You for instructing St. Faustina not only to write about Your mercy toward sinners but also to beg for mercy for them.

Be Not Afraid

Today, I have heard these words: **My daughter, delight of My Heart, it is with pleasure that I look into your soul. I bestow many graces only because of you. I also withhold My punishments only because of you. You restrain Me, and I cannot vindicate the claims of My justice. You bind My hands with your love** (*Diary*, 1193).

Today I heard a voice in my soul: **Oh, if sinners knew My mercy, they would not perish in such great numbers. Tell sinful souls not to be afraid to approach Me; speak to them of My great mercy** (*Diary*, 1396).

My Prayer Response:

Lord Jesus, fill my heart with love of You like that of St. Faustina, so You may be delighted and grant many graces as I beg for mercy for souls. May many more sinners come to know of Your mercy while it is still time for mercy.

A Burning Desire to Save Souls

The Lord said to me, **The loss of each soul plunges Me into mortal sadness. You always console Me when you pray for sinners. The prayer most pleasing to Me is prayer for the conversion of sinners. Know, My daughter, that this prayer is always heard and answered** (*Diary*, 1397).

March 25, 1938. Today, I saw the suffering Lord Jesus. He leaned down toward me and whispered softly, **My daughter, help Me to save sinners.** Suddenly, a burning desire to save souls entered my soul. When I recovered my senses, I knew just how I was to help souls, and I prepared myself for greater sufferings (*Diary*, 1645).

My Prayer Response:

Lord Jesus, I want to respond to Your "mortal sadness" caused by the loss of each soul. Give me a "burning desire to save souls" like that of St. Faustina. Give me the graces to even suffer for the conversion of sinners.

Moving Heaven

Good Friday [April 15, 1938]. I saw the Lord Jesus, tortured, but not nailed to the Cross. It was still before the crucifixion, and He said to me, **You are My Heart. Speak to sinners about My mercy.** And the Lord gave me interior knowledge of the whole abyss of His mercy for souls, and I learned that that which I had written is truly a drop (*Diary,* 1666).

I heard these words: **If you did not tie My hands, I would send down many punishments upon the earth. My daughter, your look disarms My anger. Although your lips are silent, you call out to Me so mightily that all heaven is moved. I cannot escape from your requests, because you pursue Me, not from afar but within your own heart** (*Diary,* 1722).

My Prayer Response:

Lord Jesus, through the intercession of St. Faustina, teach me how to beg for mercy on the whole world and move all of heaven like she did! Give me Your Heart, Lord, so I can appreciate better the whole abyss of Your mercy for souls.

Thrice Holy God

Write: I am Thrice Holy, and I detest the smallest sin. I cannot love a soul which is stained with sin; but when it repents, there is no limit to My generosity toward it. My mercy embraces and justifies it. With My mercy, I pursue sinners along all their paths, and My Heart rejoices when they return to Me. I forget the bitterness with which they fed My Heart and rejoice at their return (*Diary*, 1728).

The Lord said to me, **Enter into purgatory often, because they need you there.** O my Jesus, I understand the meaning of these words which You are speaking to me, but first let me enter the treasury of Your mercy (*Diary*, 1738).

My Prayer Response:

O Thrice Holy God, You detest even the smallest sin in souls. Hear my plea for Your mercy on us sinners on earth and those in purgatory. Cleanse us as we repent and return to You. May our return give You joy.

Deeds of Mercy

January 25 – 31

In a prayer to glorify the Most Holy Trinity, St. Faustina prayed that she would glorify the Holy Trinity with every breath and every beat of her heart. She asked to be transformed into mercy, praying that her eyes, ears, tongue, hands, feet, and heart be merciful.

She concluded her prayer by asking Jesus: "O my Jesus, transform me into Yourself, for You can do all things" (*Diary*, 163). It is a prayer that I love to pray every day — because I need to be transformed into His mercy.

In the midst of her prayer to be merciful, St. Faustina wrote a beautiful teaching on the three degrees or ways of showing mercy:

> You Yourself command me to exercise the three degrees of mercy. The first: the act [deed] of mercy, of whatever kind. The second: the word of mercy — if I cannot carry out a work of mercy, I will assist by my words. The third: prayer — if I cannot show mercy by deeds and words, I can always do so by prayer. My prayer reaches out even there where I cannot reach out physically (*Diary*, 163).

The Apostle of Mercy also knew that deeds of mercy must flow from a merciful heart. Thus, she prayed in these passages:

> My Jesus, make my heart like unto Your Merciful Heart (*Diary*, 692).

> Transform [my heart] into Your own Heart that I may sense the needs of other hearts, especially those who are sad and suffering (*Diary*, 514).
>
> Jesus, help me to go through life doing good to everyone (*Diary*, 692).

Like St. Faustina, let's pray for the gift of a merciful heart, so we can sense the needs of other hearts. Then deeds of mercy will become second nature to us, as mercy flows from our hearts in loving service to others — all out of love for the Lord Jesus.

The Demand for Deeds of Mercy

My daughter, if I demand through you that people revere My mercy, you should be the first to distinguish yourself by this confidence in My mercy. I demand from you deeds of mercy, which are to arise out of love for Me. You are to show mercy to your neighbors always and everywhere. You must not shrink from this or try to excuse or absolve yourself from it (*Diary*, 742).

I am giving you three ways of exercising mercy toward your neighbor: the first — by deed, the second — by word, the third— by prayer. In these three degrees is contained the fullness of mercy, and it is an unquestionable proof of love for Me. By this means a soul glorifies and pays reverence to My mercy (*Diary*, 742).

My Prayer Response:

Lord Jesus, help me to respond to Your demand for deeds of mercy. Fill me with Your love for my neighbor. Help me then to show my love for You by exercising mercy toward my neighbor in three ways: by deed, by word, and by prayer.

A Reminder of the Demands

Yes, the first Sunday after Easter is the Feast of Mercy, but there must also be acts of mercy, and I demand the worship of My mercy through the solemn celebration of the Feast and through the veneration of the image which is painted. By means of this image I shall grant many graces to souls. It is to be a reminder of the demands of My mercy, because even the strongest faith is of no avail without works (*Diary*, 742).

My Prayer Response with St. Faustina:

O my Jesus, You Yourself must help me in everything, because You see how very little I am, and so I depend solely on Your goodness, O God (*Diary*, 742).

Deeds Done for Me

The doctor did not allow me to go to the chapel to attend the Passion Service, although I had a great desire for it; however, I prayed in my own room. Suddenly I heard the bell in the next room, and I went in and rendered a service to a seriously sick person. When I returned to my room, I suddenly saw the Lord Jesus, who said, **My daughter, you gave Me greater pleasure by rendering Me that service than if you had prayed for a long time.** I answered, "But it was not to You, Jesus, but to that patient that I rendered this service." And the Lord answered me, **Yes, My daughter, but whatever you do for your neighbor, you do for Me** (*Diary*, 1029).

My Prayer Response:

Thank You, Jesus, for teaching us through St. Faustina: **Whatever you do for your neighbor, you do for Me** (see Mt 25:40). Help us, Lord Jesus, to respond with deeds of mercy whenever You appear in the disguise of the needy, as did Blessed Mother Teresa of Calcutta.

Our Task

September 6, 1937. Today, I begin a new assignment. I go from the garden to the desert of the gate. I went in to talk to the Lord for a while. I asked Him for a blessing and for graces to faithfully carry out the duties entrusted to me. I heard these words: **My daughter, I am always with you. I have given you the opportunity to practice deeds of mercy which you will perform according to obedience. You will give Me much pleasure if, each evening, you will speak to Me especially about this task.** I felt that Jesus had given me a new grace in relation to my new duties; but, despite this, I have locked myself deeper in His Heart (*Diary*, 1267).

My Prayer Response:

Jesus, please give me opportunities to practice deeds of mercy. Open my eyes and ears to the needs of those around me. And lead me deeper into Your Heart of love and mercy for all.

Spiritual Mercy

I understand Your words, Lord, and the magnitude of the mercy that ought to shine in my soul. Jesus: **I know, My daughter, that you understand it and that you do everything within your power. But write this for the many souls who are often worried because they do not have the material means with which to carry out an act of mercy. Yet spiritual mercy, which requires neither permissions nor storehouses, is much more meritorious and is within the grasp of every soul. If a soul does not exercise mercy somehow or other, it will not obtain My mercy on the day of judgment** (*Diary*, 1317).

My Prayer Response:

My Jesus, thank You for teaching us through St. Faustina about "spiritual mercies" when we do not have material goods to give. We can always encourage others by our word, by our prayer, and by our kindness — and especially by sacrifice lovingly accomplished, which You, Jesus, called **exercising mercy in spirit** (*Diary*, 1316).

Be Always Merciful

[After St. Faustina fed a poor young man a bowl of soup, she writes:]

As I was taking the bowl from him, he gave me to know that He was the Lord of heaven and earth. … I heard these words in my soul: **My daughter, the blessings of the poor who bless Me as they leave this gate have reached My ears. And your compassion, within the bounds of obedience, has pleased Me, and this is why I came down from My throne — to taste the fruits of your mercy** (*Diary*, 1312).

Then I heard the words, **I am glad you behaved like My true daughter. Be always merciful as I am merciful. Love everyone out of love for Me, even your greatest enemies, so that My mercy may be fully reflected in your heart** (*Diary*, 1695).

My Prayer Response:

Lord Jesus, help me to "be merciful just as Your Father is merciful" (Lk 6:36). May I always be merciful — always, everywhere, and to everyone.

Pray for Your Enemies

My daughter, in this meditation, consider the love of neighbor. Is your love for your neighbor guided by My love? Do you pray for your enemies? Do you wish well to those who have, in one way or another, caused you sorrow or offended you?

Know that whatever good you do to any soul, I accept it as if you had done it to Me (*Diary*, 1768).

My Prayer Response:

Lord Jesus, help me to pray for my enemies and for those who have caused me sorrows. Teach me to live Your word: "Whatever you did for one of these least brothers of Mine, you did for Me" (Mt 25:40).

Spiritual Directors and Confessors

February 1 – 16

In his remarkable book *The Fulfillment of All Desire*, Ralph Martin shares the wisdom of the Doctors of the Church who are masters of the spiritual life: Saints Teresa of Avila, John of the Cross, Bernard of Clairvaux, Francis de Sales, Therese of Lisieux, Augustine of Hippo, and Catherine of Siena (Emmaus Road Publishing, Steubenville, OH, 2007). The author summarizes their advice about spiritual directors in the words of St. Francis de Sales:

> Do you seriously wish to travel the road to devotion? If so, look for a good man to guide and lead you. This is the most important of all words of advice *(The Fulfillment of All Desire*, p. 265; from *Introduction to the Devout Life*, I, 4).

Because it is not always possible to find a priest as a spiritual director, I summarize the advice of the Doctors of the Church in this way: Find a mature spiritual man or woman as a friend and guide. A mature spiritual guide knows and experiences the presence of the Lord and has some knowledge of the spiritual journey. Such a guide can recognize the movements of the Holy Spirit's activity in a person's life.

Also, even if you can't find a priest to be your spiritual director, you can decide to go regularly to confession to a particular priest. He can help guide you spiritually by getting a good sense of the sorts of sins and weaknesses that you struggle with.

In her *Diary*, St. Faustina describes how the Lord

Jesus guided her through the spiritual director and confessor He gave her:

> On, how wretched my soul is for having wasted so many graces! I was running away from God, and He pursued me with His graces. I most often experienced God's graces when I least expected them, From the moment He gave me a spiritual director, I have been more faithful to grace. Thanks to the director and his watchfulness over my soul, I have learned what guidance means and how Jesus looks at it. Jesus warned me of the least fault and stressed that He Himself judges the matter that I present to my confessor; and [He told me] that ... **any transgressions against the confessor touch Me Myself. ...**
>
> [Jesus] tells me to ask my confessor about everything and often says, **I will answer You through His mouth. Be at peace.** It has never happened to me that I have received an answer which was contrary to what the Lord wanted of me, when I presented it to the spiritual director [Fr. Michael Sopocko] (*Diary*, 145).

Two priests guided Sr. Faustina. As Sr. Faustina's spiritual director in Vilnius (part of Poland during Sr. Faustina's life), Fr. Michael Sopocko ordered her to write her *Diary*. He would then study it when he had time, since he was busy as a university professor of theology. (On September 28, 2008, Fr. Sopocko was declared blessed by the Church.) Before Sr. Faustina went to Vilnius, she received spiritual direction from Fr. Joseph Andrasz, SJ, in Krakow. As we shall see in the *Diary* passages that follow, Jesus chose both of these priests to help guide Sr. Faustina. And He chose Fr. Sopocko in a special way to help her fulfill her mission of mercy for the world.

Visible Help on Earth

… the goodness of Jesus is infinite; He had promised me visible help here on earth, and a little while later I received it in Vilnius, in the person of Father Sopocko. I had already known him before coming to Vilnius, thanks to an interior vision. One day I saw him in our chapel between the altar and the confessional and suddenly heard a voice in my soul say, **This is the visible help for you on earth. He will help you carry out My will on earth** (*Diary*, 53).

Write that by day and by night My gaze is fixed upon [Fr. Sopocko] **and I permit these adversities in order to increase his merit. I do not reward for good results but for the patience and hardship undergone for My sake** (*Diary*, 86).

My Prayer Response:

Lord Jesus, thank You for providing a spiritual director for St. Faustina. Thank You that, through his direction, she wrote her *Diary*. We have before us Your words to her and her responses that speak to us now. They are the fruit of St. Faustina's obedience to her spiritual director.

Be Totally Open

✝ Before confession, I heard these words in my soul, **My daughter, tell him everything and reveal your soul to him as you do before Me. Do not fear anything. It is to keep you in peace that I place this priest between your soul and Myself. The words he will speak to you are My words. Reveal to him your soul's greatest secrets. I will give him light to know your soul** (*Diary*, 232).

My Prayer Response:

Thank You, Lord Jesus, for directing St. Faustina to be totally open with her spiritual director. The fruit of her relationship with You and her spiritual director is found in her saintly life and is written in her *Diary*.

Like a Child towards Him

In the evening, the Lord said to me, **My daughter, let nothing frighten or disconcert you. Remain deeply at peace. Everything is in My hands. I will give you to understand everything through Father Andrasz. Be like a child towards him** (*Diary*, 219).

My Prayer Response:

Thank You, Lord, for Father Andrasz who would not allow St. Faustina to turn away from her interior inspirations and her work of promoting the message of Divine Mercy (see *Diary*, 52-53). He insisted on humility, humility, humility (see *Diary* 54-55). Through a good spiritual guide, Lord, teach me humility.

Value in Suffering for Jesus

I saw that God Himself seemed to be opposing [Fr. Sopocko], and I asked the Lord why He was acting in this way toward him, as though He were placing obstacles in the way of his doing what He Himself had asked him to do. And the Lord said, **I am acting thus with him to give testimony that this work is Mine. Tell him not to fear anything; My gaze is on him day and night. There will be as many crowns to form his crown as there will be souls saved by this work. It is not for the success of a work, but for the suffering that I give reward** (*Diary*, 90).

My Prayer Response:

Thank You, Lord, for supporting Fr. Sopocko in the work of promoting Your mercy. Thank You for the faithfulness of Fr. Sopocko in the midst of sufferings he encountered in this work of Divine Mercy. Thank You for the support of St. Faustina's prayers for Fr. Sopocko. As You guided St. Faustina and Fr. Sopocko, guide me, Lord, in spreading the message of Your mercy.

I Will Not Leave You

✝ That evening, I remained in the chapel a little longer. I talked to the Lord about a certain soul. Encouraged by His goodness, I said, "Jesus, You gave me this Father who understands my inspirations, and now You are taking him away from me again. What am I going to do in this Vilnius? I don't know anyone there, and even the dialect of the people there is foreign to me." And the Lord said to me, **Do not fear; I will not leave you to yourself.** My soul drowned itself in a prayer of thanksgiving for all the graces that the Lord had granted me through the mediation of Father Andrasz.

Suddenly, I remembered the vision in which I had seen that priest between the confessional and the altar, trusting that I would meet him [Fr. Sopocko] some day. And the words I had heard came back vividly: **He will help you to fulfill My will here on earth** (*Diary*, 258).

My Prayer Response:

Lord Jesus, thank You for providing two holy and knowledgeable priests as spiritual directors to St. Faustina.

Deep Peace Filled My Soul

Once, when I had finished a novena to the Holy Spirit for the intention of my confessor [Father Sopocko], the Lord answered, **I made him known to you even before your superiors had sent you here. As you will act towards your confessor, so I will act toward you. If you conceal something from him, even though it be the least of My graces, I too will hide Myself from you, and you will remain alone.** And so I followed God's wish, and a deep peace filled my soul. Now I understand how the Lord defends confessors and how He protects them (*Diary*, 269).

My Prayer Response:

Lord Jesus, bless and guide our confessors and spiritual directors with Your Holy Spirit. May they recognize the action of the Holy Spirit in our lives. Keep us humble and open with our confessors and spiritual directors.

The Grace of Complete Confidence

I heard these words in my soul: **I want you to be open and simple as a child with My representative** [Father Andrasz] **just as you are with Me; otherwise I will leave you and will not commune with you.**

Truly, God gave me the great grace of complete confidence, and after the conversation, God granted me the grace of deep peace and light concerning these matters (*Diary*, 494).

My Prayer Response:

Lord Jesus, may I always be open and simple as a child with Your representative. May I "speak the truth in love" (Eph 4:15). Grant me the grace of confidence in Your representative.

Our Weakness

I saw Jesus in the usual way, and He spoke these words to me: **Lay your head on My shoulder, rest and regain your strength. I am always with you. Tell the friend of My Heart** [Fr. Andrasz] **that I use such feeble creatures to carry out My work.** After a while my spirit was strengthened with great power. **Tell him that I had let him see your weakness during your confession to show him what you are of yourself** (*Diary*, 498).

My Prayer Response:

Thank You, Jesus, that in revealing our weakness in confession and spiritual direction, You make known what we are without Your grace. You use our very misery to make known Your great mercy.

Rely on Your Confessor

Thursday. During the evening adoration, I saw Jesus scourged and tortured. He said to me, **My daughter, I desire that even in the smallest things, you rely on your confessor. Your greatest sacrifices do not please Me if you practice them without the confessor's permission** (*Diary*, 639).

My Prayer Response:

Lord Jesus, help me to rely on my confessor in even the smallest things. Help me to open my heart to him and seek his counsel — all out of obedience to You.

Do Nothing out of Self-Will

The greatest works are worthless in My eyes if they are done out of self-will, and often they are not in accord with My will and merit punishment rather than reward. And on the other hand, even the smallest of your acts, done with the confessor's permission is pleasing in My eyes and very dear to Me. Hold firmly to this always. Be constantly on the watch, for many souls will turn back from the gates of hell and worship My mercy. But fear nothing, as I am with you. Know that of yourself you can do nothing (*Diary*, 639).

My Prayer Response:

Lord Jesus, keep me on the watch for sacrifices to offer to You for the salvation of souls. I surrender my will to You. For without You, I can do nothing of value. To help me in taking up this charge, give me a good confessor to guide me.

The Seal of Obedience

I became absorbed in prayer and said my penance. Then I suddenly saw the Lord, who said to me, **My daughter, know that you give Me greater glory by a single act of obedience than by long prayers and mortifications.** Oh, how good it is to live under obedience, to live conscious of the fact that everything I do is pleasing to God! (*Diary*, 894).

I heard the following words in my soul: **You will receive a greater reward for your obedience and subjection to your confessor than you will for the practices which you will be carrying out. Know this, My daughter, and act accordingly: anything, no matter how small it be, that has the seal of obedience to My representative is pleasing to Me and great in My eyes** (*Diary*, 933).

My Prayer Response:

Lord Jesus, thank You for teaching me about obedience to Your representative in the confessional. Help me with Your grace to submit to Your will expressed by Your representative. Teach me the importance of an obedient spirit to those you place in spiritual authority over me.

I Speak through Him

I saw Jesus, and He spoke these words to me: **Be obedient to your director in everything; his word is My will. Be certain in the depths of your soul that it is I who am speaking through his lips, and I desire that you reveal the state of your soul to him with the same simplicity and candor as you have with Me. I say it again, My daughter: know that his word is My will for you** (*Diary*, 979).

My Prayer Response:

Thank You, Jesus, for Your teaching to St. Faustina about obedience to her spiritual director: **Know that his word is My will for you.** May I hear Your word through my spiritual director or confessor and act upon it.

A Priest after My Own Heart

[August 30, 1937] Reverend Father Sopocko left this morning. When I was steeped in a prayer of thanksgiving for the great grace that I had received from God; namely, that of seeing Father, [Jesus said to me,] **He is a priest after My own Heart; his efforts are pleasing to Me. You see, My daughter, that My will must be done and that which I had promised you, I shall do. Through him I spread comfort to suffering and care-worn souls. Through him it pleased Me to proclaim the worship of My mercy. And through this work of mercy more souls will come close to Me than otherwise would have, even if he had kept giving absolution day and night for the rest of his life, because by so doing, he would have labored only for as long as he lived; whereas, thanks to this work of mercy, he will be laboring till the end of the world** (*Diary*, 1256).

My Prayer Response:

Lord Jesus, thank You for choosing Fr. Sopocko to proclaim the worship of Your mercy. Guide me in sharing with others about Your mercy.

He Is the Veil

✞ Jesus, I have noticed that You seem to be less concerned with me. **Yes, My child, I am replacing Myself with your spiritual director** [Father Andrasz]. **He is taking care of you according to My will. Respect his every word as My own. He is the veil behind which I am hiding. Your director and I are one; his words are My words** (*Diary*, 1308).

My Prayer Response:

Thank You, Lord Jesus, for explaining to St. Faustina and so to me how You relate to St. Faustina's spiritual director: He is the veil behind which You are hiding; You are one with him; his words are Your words. Please be one with my spiritual director or confessor.

Be at Peace

I was present at Holy Mass celebrated by Father Sopocko. During the Mass, I saw the Infant Jesus who, touching the priest's forehead with His finger, said to me, **His thought is closely united to Mine, so be at peace about what concerns My work. I will not let him make a mistake, and you should do nothing without his permission.** This filled my soul with great peace as regards everything that has to do with this work (*Diary*, 1408).

My Prayer Response:

Lord Jesus, thank You for the confidence You expressed in Fr. Sopocko's thoughts being united with Yours. It gave St. Faustina great peace about her work of mercy. May I, too, experience Your peace in proclaiming Your mercy in response to the encouragement of my spiritual director or confessor.

Boundless Sincerity

And now I am going to tell you something that is most important for you: Boundless sincerity with your spiritual director. If you do not take advantage of this great grace according to My instructions, I will take him away from you, and then you will be left to yourself; and all the torments, which you know very well, will return to you. It displeases Me that you do not take advantage of the opportunity when you are able to see him and talk with him. Know that it is a great grace on My part when I give a spiritual director to a soul. Many souls ask Me for this, but it is not to all that I grant this grace. From the moment when I gave you this priest as spiritual director, I endowed him with new light so that he might easily know and understand your soul (*Diary*, 1561).

My Prayer Response:

Lord Jesus, thank You for the gift of my spiritual director or confessor. May I have "boundless sincerity" with him. Please bless him with Your presence, protection, and peace. I pray for good spiritual directors and confessors for all those in need of guidance in the spiritual life.

The Image of The Divine Mercy

February 17 – 24

The revelation of Jesus as The Divine Mercy is the first revelation that St. Faustina recorded in her *Diary* (see 47-48). Jesus expressed His desire that The Divine mercy image with the signature "Jesus, I trust in You!" be venerated throughout the world, especially on the Feast of Mercy. Jesus told St. Faustina, **I am offering people a vessel with which they are to keep coming for graces to the fountain of mercy. That vessel is this image with thc signature: "Jesus, I trust in You"** (*Diary*, 327).

I consider the painted image of the Merciful Jesus as an *icon* in the Western style, because it portrays the inner or deeper reality that is essential to the purpose of an icon: showing *divine light radiating out of darkness* within. One might call such an icon or sacred image a window on heavenly realities. In the case of The Divine Mercy image, it is also the essential icon of Christ since it points to the whole paschal or Easter mystery of our salvation: the Passion, death, and Resurrection of Jesus (see *Spirit of the Liturgy* by Cardinal Joseph Ratzinger, now Pope Benedict XVI).

Saint Faustina recorded her vision of Jesus as The Divine Mercy in her cell in Plock, Poland:

> February 22, 1931. In the evening, when I was in my cell, I saw the Lord Jesus clothed in a white garment. One hand [was] raised in the gesture of blessing, the other was touching the garment at the breast. From beneath

> the garment, slightly drawn aside at the breast, there were emanating two large rays, one red, the other pale. In silence I kept my gaze fixed on the Lord; my soul was struck with awe, but also with great joy (*Diary*, 47).

In cooperation with her spiritual director, Fr. Michael Sopocko, Sr. Faustina described her vision of the Merciful Jesus to the artist Eugene Kazimirowski in Vilnius. She made regular visits to his studio to see his progress. The finished painting was then first displayed on the Feast of Divine Mercy, April 28, 1935, at the Shrine of Our Lady of Mercy (*Ostra Brama*) in Vilnius. The occasion marked the close of the Jubilee Year of the Redemption of the World.

In this section, let the words of Jesus to St. Faustina encourage you to honor and venerate The Divine Mercy image of your choice. Enthrone the image of the Merciful Jesus as a reminder to draw graces from the fountain of mercy.

Place the image of Jesus in a prominent place in your home, your workplace, and in your car. Get a holy card with it, so you can carry the image with you and use it as a bookmark for your spiritual reading.

The Pattern That You See

Paint an image according to the pattern you see, with the signature: Jesus, I trust in You. I desire that this image be venerated, first in your chapel, and [then] **throughout the world** (*Diary*, 47).

My Prayer Response

Jesus, I adore You portrayed in this image as The Divine Mercy. I thank You for revealing this powerful image of Yourself to St. Faustina. May many souls venerate this image as a way of expressing their trust in You. Jesus, I trust in You!

At the Hour of Death

I promise that the soul that will venerate this image will not perish. I also promise victory over [its] **enemies already here on earth, especially at the hour of death. I Myself will defend it as My own glory** (*Diary*, 48).

My Prayer Response:

Jesus, I rely on Your promises as I venerate Your image — that You will defend me in the battle of life and especially at the hour of my death. I pray for a special grace of Your mercy for all those who are in spiritual peril and for those who are dying.

The Depth of My Mercy

I will make this all clear to the superior by means of the graces which I will grant through this image (*Diary*, 51).

I desire that this image be displayed in public on the first Sunday after Easter. That Sunday is the Feast of Mercy. Through the Word Incarnate, I make known the bottomless depth of My mercy (*Diary*, 88).

My Prayer Response:

Jesus, through the image of You as The Divine Mercy, make known to me the infinite depth of Your Mercy. May this image be displayed in public on Divine Mercy Sunday in every church throughout the world.

A Shield and Shelter

The two rays denote Blood and Water. The pale ray stands for the Water which makes souls righteous. The red ray stands for the Blood which is the life of souls. …

These two rays issued forth from the very depths of My tender mercy when My agonized Heart was opened by a lance on the Cross.

These rays shield souls from the wrath of My Father. Happy is the one who will dwell in their shelter, for the just hand of God shall not lay hold of him (*Diary*, 299).

My Prayer Response:

May the Blood and Water that gushed forth from Your Heart, Jesus, shield and shelter me with Your mercy. Then the just hand of God shall not lay hold of me.

In My Grace

Know that if you neglect the matter of the painting of the image and the whole work of mercy, you will have to answer for a multitude of souls on the day of judgment (*Diary*, 154).

Not in the beauty of the color, nor of the brush lies the greatness of this image, but in My grace (*Diary*, 313).

My Prayer Response:

Jesus, by the grace that flows from Your image, strengthen and inspire me to proclaim Your mercy to many. Remind me always that the greatness of this image lies in Your grace.

A Vessel for Graces

Once, Jesus said to me, **My gaze from this image is like My gaze from the cross** (*Diary*, 326).

I am offering people a vessel with which they are to keep coming for graces to the fountain of mercy. That vessel is this image with the signature: "Jesus, I trust in You" (*Diary*, 327).

My Prayer Response:

Jesus, look at me from the cross, so I may trust in You even more each time I gaze at You portrayed in Your image. I want to keep coming to this image as a vessel for graces. Keep my gaze fixed on You.

Witness to Your Mercy

I desire that the image be publicly honored (*Diary*, 414).

[After seeing the image come alive, I heard these words,] **You are a witness of My mercy. You shall stand before My throne forever as a living witness to My mercy** (*Diary*, 417).

My Prayer Response:

Jesus, as I honor Your image as The Divine Mercy, inspire me to witness to Your mercy. May I stand before Your throne forever as a living witness to Your mercy.

Rays of Mercy

These rays of mercy will pass through you, just as they have passed through this Host, and they will go out through all the world (*Diary*, 441).

Already there are many souls who have been drawn to My love by this image. My mercy acts in souls through this work (*Diary*, 1379).

My Prayer Response:

Jesus, may the rays of Your mercy pass through me to many souls in need. I desire that these rays of mercy draw more souls to Your love.

Misery

February 25 – March 3

One of my favorite entries in St. Faustina's *Diary* is passage 1318. Over the years in giving retreats and conferences on The Divine Mercy message and devotion, I've recited this key text from memory. At conferences, I've also asked literally thousands of people to respond by a show of hands if they have experienced misery in their lives. Interestingly, I've never yet met an adult with no miseries. How about you?

Listen to this conversation between St. Faustina and the Lord Jesus in this main passage on misery:

> October 10, [1937]. O my Jesus, in thanksgiving for Your many graces, I offer You my body and soul, intellect and will, and all the sentiments of my heart. Through the vows, I have given myself entirely to You; I have then nothing more that I can offer You. Jesus said to me, **My daughter, you have not offered Me that which is really yours.** I probed deeply into myself and found that I love God with all the faculties of my soul and, unable to see what it was that I had not yet given to the Lord, I asked, "Jesus, tell me what it is, and I will give it to You at once with a generous heart." Jesus said to me with kindness, **Daughter, give Me your misery, because it is your exclusive property.** At that moment, a ray of light illumined my soul, and I saw the whole abyss of my misery. In that same moment, I nestled close to the Most Sacred

> Heart of Jesus with so much trust that even if I had the sins of all the damned weighing on my conscience, I would not have doubted God's mercy but, with heart crushed to dust, I would have thrown myself into the abyss of Your mercy. I believe, O Jesus, that You would not reject me, but would absolve me through the hand of Your representative (*Diary*, 1318).

Notice what Jesus tells St. Faustina, **Give Me your misery, because it is your exclusive property.** Notice, too, how the great Apostle of Mercy then responds with great trust in the Lord Jesus as she sees the whole abyss of her misery.

Inspired by St. Faustina's example, may these *Diary* entries on misery encourage you to offer all of your troubles and miseries of every day and every moment to the Lord. Trust in Him and release them all to Him. He is a like a garbage collector who transforms the refuse we give Him — all for the salvation of souls!

Consume Our Miseries

Be at peace, My daughter, it is precisely through such misery that I want to show the power of My mercy (*Diary*, 133).

My daughter, all your miseries have been consumed in the flame of My love, like a little twig thrown into a roaring fire. By humbling yourself in this way, you draw upon yourself and upon other souls an entire sea of My mercy (*Diary*, 178).

My Prayer Response:

Lord Jesus, consume our miseries in the flame of Your merciful love. May our humble submission to You draw upon us and upon other souls an entire sea of Your mercy.

Complete Trust

After Holy Communion, I heard these words — **You see what you are of yourself, but do not be frightened at this. If I were to reveal to you the whole misery that you are, you would die of terror. However, be aware of what you are. Because you are such great misery, I have revealed to you the whole ocean of My mercy. I seek and desire souls like yours, but they are few. Your great trust in Me forces Me to continuously grant you graces. You have great and incomprehensible rights over My Heart, for you are a daughter of complete trust. You would not have been able to bear the magnitude of the love which I have for you if I had revealed it to you fully here on earth** (*Diary*, 718).

My Prayer Response:

Saint Faustina, pray for us that we may trust like you. May our great trust in Jesus open for us a whole treasury of graces.

The Greater the Sinner

Today, I heard these words: **The graces I grant you are not for you alone, but for a great number of other souls as well. … And your heart is My constant dwelling place, despite the misery that you are. I unite Myself with you, take away your misery, and give you My mercy. I perform works of mercy in every soul. The greater the sinner, the greater the right he has to My mercy. My mercy is confirmed in every work of My hands. He who trusts in My mercy will not perish, for all his affairs are Mine, and his enemies will be shattered at the base of My footstool** (*Diary*, 723).

My Prayer Response:

Lord Jesus, work miracles of mercy in the souls of the miserable, especially those trapped in sin, because they so need Your mercy. Help us all to trust in Your mercy.

Only with Your Help

Today, I heard these words: **You see how weak you are, so when shall I be able to count on you?** (*Diary*, 722).

Without special help from Me, you are not even capable of accepting My graces. You know who you are (*Diary*, 738).

My daughter, you have not offered Me that which is really yours. … Daughter, give Me your misery, because it is your exclusive property (*Diary*, 1318).

My Prayer Response

Lord Jesus, You know my misery. I cannot even accept Your graces of mercy without help from You. Jesus, help me to trust in You and accept Your mercy.

Nothing But Misery

My daughter, what you have said is true. You are very miserable, and it pleased Me to carry out this work of mercy precisely through you who are nothing but misery itself. Do not fear; I will not leave you alone. Do whatever you can in this matter; I will accomplish everything that is lacking in you. You know what is within your power to do; do that (*Diary*, 881).

My Prayer Response:

Jesus, in my misery help me to trust in You. Help me to accept Your graces and do what is in my power to do. Jesus, I trust in You!

Nothing Will Stop Me

Today the Lord said to me, **My daughter, My pleasure and delight, nothing will stop Me from granting you graces. Your misery does not hinder My mercy. My daughter, write that the greater the misery of a soul, the greater its right to My mercy; [urge] all souls to trust in the unfathomable abyss of My mercy, because I want to save them all. On the cross, the fountain of My mercy was opened wide by the lance for all souls — no one have I excluded!** (*Diary*, 1182).

My Prayer Response:

Thank You, Jesus, that nothing will stop You from granting me Your graces. I rely on Your Heart opened on the cross to bathe me in Your mercy. Bathe me and the whole world in Your mercy!

Distressed Souls

Write this for the benefit of distressed souls; when a soul sees and realizes the gravity of its sins, when the whole abyss of the misery into which it immersed itself is displayed before its eyes, let it not despair, but with trust let it throw itself into the arms of My mercy, as a child into the arms of its beloved mother. These souls have a right of priority to My compassionate Heart, they have first access to My mercy. Tell them that no soul that has called upon My mercy has been disappointed or brought to shame. I delight particularly in a soul which has placed its trust in My goodness (*Diary*, 1541).

My Prayer Response:

Jesus, I pray for distressed souls — plunge them into the ocean of Your mercy. Help them to trust in Your goodness! May trusting souls delight You.

Offer Me Your Misery

Write, My daughter, that I am mercy itself for the contrite soul. A soul's greatest wretchedness does not enkindle Me with wrath; but rather, My Heart is moved towards it with great mercy (*Diary*, 1739).

For you, I am mercy itself; therefore I ask you to offer Me your misery and this very helplessness of yours and, in this way, you will delight My Heart (*Diary*, 1775).

My Prayer Response:

Jesus, You are mercy itself. I offer You my misery and that of the whole world. May Your Heart of Mercy delight at this offering of our misery to You. Jesus, have mercy on us and on the whole world.

Do Not Fear; I Am with You

March 4 – 21

Working on the theme of "Do not fear; I am with you" was a time of revelation for me! It was a deeper insight on misery in the life of St. Faustina and that of my own. I realized that when she described herself as an "abyss of misery," it was not a pious exaggeration. She really knew what she was without God's mercy (see *Diary*, 1318 and 1734).

Saint Faustina discovered that her real miseries were primarily fears: fears of deception, fears of inadequacy, and fears of attacks. But, with the grace of the Lord's presence, she grew in trust and so was at peace. She also began to discern Jesus' purpose more clearly. Saint Faustina began to see that her response to her miseries of fears, sickness, and other types of suffering proved a great source of grace for the conversion of sinners and the salvation of souls as she placed all her trust in the Lord Jesus.

The insight into my own life was that the miseries of my anxieties and ailments are the "raw material" that the Lord wants to use for the salvation of souls as I offer them to Him. So, the repeated words of our Lord to St. Faustina apply to me and to you as well:

> Do not fear — trust in Me even more.
>
> I am with you — always, because I love you.

I'm learning from St. Faustina that the more miseries I experience and the more I trust in Jesus, the more I grow spiritually and the more souls benefit from the

Lord's mercy flowing through me to them. However, this is a challenging lesson to learn. I find that the Lord needs to repeat this teaching to me as He did to St. Faustina, over and over again.

As you reflect on the words of Jesus on the theme of "Do not fear; I am with you," may you, too, learn this important spiritual lesson and put your miseries to good use.

Filled with a Certain Strength

Suddenly I saw the Lord interiorly, and He said to me, **Fear not, My daughter; I am with you.** In that single moment, all the darkness and torments vanished, my senses were inundated with unspeakable joy, [and] the faculties of my soul filled with light (*Diary*, 103).

Satan always takes advantage of such moments; thoughts of discouragement began to rise to the surface — for your faithfulness and sincerity — this is your reward. How can one be sincere when one is so misunderstood? Jesus, Jesus, I cannot go on any longer. Again I fell to the ground under this weight, and I broke out in a sweat, and fear began to overcome me. I had no one to lean on interiorly. Suddenly I heard a voice within my soul, **Do not fear; I am with you.** And an unusual light illumined my mind, and I understood that I should not give in to such sorrows. I was filled with a certain strength and left my cell with new courage to suffer (*Diary*, 129).

My Prayer Response:

Lord Jesus, help me to hear Your word of encouragement when I need it: **Do not fear; I am with you.**

Profound Peace

I have wasted many of God's graces because I was always afraid of being deluded. God drew me to Himself so powerfully that often it was not in my power to resist His grace when I was suddenly immersed in Him. At these moments, Jesus filled me with such great peace that, later on, even when I tried to become uneasy, I could not do so. And then, I heard these words in my soul: **In order that you may be assured that it is I who am demanding all these things of you, I will give you such profound peace that even if you wanted to feel troubled and frightened, it would not be in your power to do so today, but love will flood your soul to the point of self-oblivion** (*Diary*, 143).

Jesus looked at me kindly and said, **My daughter, do not be afraid of sufferings; I am with you** (*Diary*, 151).

My Prayer Response:

Lord Jesus, in Your great mercy, help me to respond to my troubles with trust! Give me profound peace that will dispel my fears.

As a Little Child

Once, when I was deeply moved by the thought of eternity and its mysteries, my soul became fearful; and when I pondered about these a little longer, I started to be troubled by various doubts. Then Jesus said to me, My child, do not be afraid of the house of your Father. Leave these vain inquiries to the wise of this world. I want to see you always as a little child. Ask your confessor about everything with simplicity, and I will answer you through his lips (*Diary*, 290).

My daughter, have fear of nothing; I am always with you. All your adversaries will harm you only to the degree that I permit them to do so. You are my dwelling place and my constant repose. For your sake I will withhold the hand which punishes; for your sake I bless the earth (*Diary*, 431).

My Prayer Response:

Lord Jesus, with childlike simplicity, may I always trust in You. I will then watch with delight to see how You work things out in Your providence.

Why Are You Fearful?

On one occasion, the Lord said to me, **Why are you fearful and why do you tremble when you are united to Me? I am displeased when a soul yields to vain terrors. Who will dare to touch you when you are with Me? Most dear to Me is the soul that strongly believes in My goodness and has complete trust in Me. I heap My confidence upon it and give it all it asks** (*Diary*, 453).

On one occasion, I felt an urge to set to work and fulfill whatever God is demanding of me. I entered the chapel for a moment and heard a voice in my soul saying, **Why are you afraid? Do you think that I will not have enough omnipotence to support you?** At that moment, my soul felt extraordinary strength, and all the adversities that could befall me in carrying out God's will seemed as nothing to me (*Diary*, 527).

My Prayer Response:

Lord Jesus, I trust in Your omnipotence to care for me. Give me strength when I am fearful and question Your love and mercy.

A Great Interior Calm

I heard these words in my soul: **Do not fear anything, I am with you. These matters are in My hands and I will bring them to fruition according to My mercy, for nothing can oppose My will** (*Diary,* 573).

Do not fear anything; I am always with you (*Diary,* 613).

Do not fear anything, My daughter; all the adversaries will be shattered at My feet. At these words, a deep peace and a great interior calm entered my soul (*Diary,* 626).

My Prayer Response:

Jesus, dearest Savior, thank You for repeating over and over again what I need to hear so often: **Fear not; I am with you.** And You add so tenderly: **I love you.**

In New Situations

[When St. Faustina was assigned to a different house, she wrote:]

When I complained to the Lord that He was taking my help away and that I would be alone again and would not know what to do, I heard these words: **Do not be afraid; I am always with you** (*Diary*, 627).

When I entered the chapel for a moment that same evening, to thank God for all the graces He had bestowed on me in this house, suddenly God's presence enveloped me. I felt like a child in the hands of the best of fathers, and I heard these words: **Do not fear anything. I am always with you** (*Diary*, 629).

March 22, [1936]. When I arrived at Warsaw, … I submitted myself in all things to His holy will. I heard these words: **Fear nothing; all difficulties will serve for the fulfillment of My will** (*Diary*, 634).

My Prayer Response:

Lord Jesus, when a new situation enters my life, may I hear Your consoling words: **Fear not; I am with you.**

Special Grace

Then suddenly Jesus stood by me and said, **Where are you intending to go?** (*Diary*, 673).

I gave no answer to Jesus, but poured out all my sorrow before Him, and Satan's attempts ceased. Jesus then said to me, **The inner peace that you have is a grace,** and suddenly He was gone. I felt happy and unaccountably peaceful. Really, for so much peace to return within a moment — that is a thing only Jesus can do, He, the most high Lord (*Diary*, 674).

Thursday. Although I was very tired today, I nevertheless resolved to make a Holy Hour. I could not pray, nor could I remain kneeling, but I remained in prayer for a whole hour and united myself in spirit with those souls who are already worshiping God in the perfect way. [Then Jesus said to me,] **Your prayer is extremely pleasing to Me** (*Diary*, 691).

My Prayer Response:

Lord Jesus, when temptations are attacking me and fatigue is exhausting me, grant me Your peace. Give me the special grace of Your mercy.

I Overcome Your Difficulties

November 19, [1936]. During Mass today, I saw the Lord Jesus, who said to me, **Be at peace, My daughter; I see your efforts, which are very pleasing to Me** (*Diary*, 757).

As I was conversing with the hidden God, He gave me to see and understand that I should not be reflecting so much and building up fear of the difficulties which I might encounter. **Know that I am with you; I bring about the difficulties, and I overcome them; in one instant, I can change a hostile disposition to one which is favorable to this cause.** The Lord explained many things to me in today's dialogue, although I am not putting everything in writing (*Diary*, 788).

My Prayer Response:

Lord Jesus, help me with Your peace to overcome anxieties and not to dwell on the difficulties of my work. Be my peace and victory.

In Seclusion

[Sister Faustina wrote the following when she was being sent to the Sanatorium for her tuberculosis.]

When I was somewhat overcome by the fear that I was to be outside the community for so long a time alone, Jesus said to me, **You will not be alone, because I am with you always and everywhere. Near to My Heart, fear nothing. I Myself am the cause of your departure. Know that My eyes follow every move of your heart with great attention. I am bringing you into seclusion so that I Myself may form your heart according to My future plans** (*Diary*, 797).

My Prayer Response:

Thank You, Jesus, for being with me when I am alone. Help me to enjoy Your presence in my heart.

What Am I Afraid of?

What are you afraid of? If you are with Me, who will dare touch you? Nevertheless, I am very pleased that you confide your fears to Me, My daughter. Speak to Me about everything in a completely simple and human way; by this you will give Me great joy. I understand you because I am God-Man. This simple language of your heart is more pleasing to Me than the hymns composed in My honor. Know, My daughter, that the simpler your speech is, the more you attract Me to yourself. And now, be at peace close to My Heart. Lay your pen aside and get ready to leave (*Diary*, 797).

My Prayer Response:

What a great question, Lord! What am I afraid of? You are always with me. Help me to be always with You.

When the Storms Rage

Then I heard the words, **Do not fear; I am with you.** When I left the altar, an extraordinary peace and power filled my soul, and the storm that was raging broke against my soul as against a rock; and the foam of the storm fell on those who had raised it. Oh, how good is the Lord, who will reward each one according to his deed! (*Diary*, 1150).

June 23, [1937]. As I was praying before the Most Blessed Sacrament, my physical sufferings ceased suddenly, and I heard this voice in my soul: **You see, I can give you everything in one moment. I am not constrained by any law.**

June 24. After Holy Communion, I heard these words: **Know, My daughter, that in one moment I can give you everything that is needed for the fulfillment of this task** (*Diary*, 1153).

My Prayer Response:

Thank You, Lord, for Your faithful word and grace when a storm of conflict or of physical suffering strikes me. In You, I am at peace.

Heavenly Protection

16 [August 1937]. After Holy Communion, I saw the Lord Jesus in all His majesty, and He said to me, **My daughter, during the weeks when you neither saw Me nor felt My presence, I was more profoundly united to you than at times** [when you experienced] **ecstasy. And the faithfulness and fragrance of your prayer have reached Me.** After these words, my soul became flooded with God's consolation (*Diary*, 1246).

When I heard how dangerous it was to be at the gate these days because of revolutionary disturbances and how many evil people have a hatred for convents, I went in and had a talk with the Lord and asked Him to so arrange it that no evil person would dare come to the gate. Then I heard these words: **My daughter, the moment you went to the gate I set a Cherub over it to guard it. Be at peace** (*Diary*, 1271).

My Prayer Response:

Jesus, You are always with me even when I do not experience You. Thank You for Your presence and protection.

Remain Faithful

My daughter, when I was before Herod, I obtained a grace for you; namely, that you would be able to rise above human scorn and follow faithfully in My footsteps. Be silent when they do not want to acknowledge your truth, because it is then that you speak more eloquently (*Diary,* 1164).

Then He said to me, **Do not fear, My child; but remain faithful only to My grace …** (*Diary,* 1166).

Today, my soul entered into close union with the Lord. He made known to me how I should always abandon myself to His holy will: **In one moment, I can give you more than you are able to desire** (*Diary,* 1169).

My Prayer Response:

Thank You, Jesus, for the grace to remain faithful and silent in times of scorn and conflict! May I always abandon myself to Your holy will.

Only a Mortal Sin

June [July] 15, 1937. Once, I learned that I was to be transferred to another house. My knowledge of this was purely interior. At the same time, I heard a voice in my soul: **Do not be afraid, My daughter; it is My will that you should remain here. Human plans will be thwarted, since they must conform to My will** (*Diary*, 1180).

When I was close to the Lord, He said to me, **Why are you afraid to begin the work which I have commanded you to carry out?** I answered, "Why do You leave me on my own at such times, Jesus, and why do I not feel Your presence?" **My daughter, even though you do not perceive Me in the most secret depths of your heart, you still cannot say that I am not there. …**

My daughter, know without doubt, and once and for all, that only mortal sin drives Me out of a soul, and nothing else (*Diary*, 1181).

My Prayer Response:

Lord Jesus, may I always be faithful to Your will, even when I am not aware of Your presence. Protect me from mortal sin that would drive You out!

Through Love and Mercy

September 25, [1937.] When I learned how great are the difficulties in this whole work, I went to the Lord and said, "Jesus, don't You see how they are hindering Your work?" And I heard a voice in my soul: **Do as much as is in your power, and don't worry about the rest. These difficulties prove that this work is Mine. Be at peace so long as you do all that is in your power** (*Diary,* 1295).

The Lord said to me, **It should be of no concern to you how anyone else acts; you are to be My living reflection, through love and mercy.** I answered, "Lord, but they often take advantage of my goodness." **That makes no difference, My daughter. That is no concern of yours. As for you, be always merciful toward other people, and especially toward sinners** (*Diary,* 1446).

My Prayer Response:

Lord Jesus, in difficulties in my work and relationships, may I rejoice and do what is in my power with peace. May I always be merciful.

Strength in Every Situation

The Lord visited me today and said, **My daughter, do not be afraid of what will happen to you. I will give you nothing beyond your strength. You know the power of My grace; let that be enough.** After these words, the Lord gave me a deeper understanding of the action of His grace (*Diary,* 1491).

January 15, 1938. Today, when the sister about whom the Lord warned me came to see me, I armed myself spiritually for battle. Although it cost me much, I did not depart one bit from what the Lord had commanded. But when an hour had gone by, and the sister made no move to go, I interiorly called upon Jesus to help. Then I heard a voice in my soul saying, **Do not fear. I am watching you this very moment and am helping you. In a moment, I will send you two sisters who are coming to visit you, and then you will find it easy to continue the conversation** (*Diary,* 1494).

My Prayer Response:

Lord Jesus, thank You for Your graces that give me strength in every situation. You watch over me every moment. Help me to always trust in You.

The Battle for Souls

Do not fear, My little child, you are not alone. Fight bravely, because My arm is supporting you; fight for the salvation of souls, exhorting them to trust in My mercy, as that is your task in this life and in the life to come. After these words, I received a deeper understanding of divine mercy. Only that soul who wants it will be damned, for God condemns no one (*Diary,* 1452).

Today I said to the Lord Jesus, "Do You see how many difficulties there are [to be overcome] before they will believe that You Yourself are the author of this work? And even now, not everyone believes in it." **Be at peace, My child; nothing can oppose My will. In spite of the murmuring and hostility of the sisters, My will shall be done in you in all its fullness, down to the last detail of My wishes and My designs** (*Diary,* 1531).

My Prayer Response:

Lord Jesus, thank You for supporting us in our battle for souls. Despite opposition to Your work, may Your will be done in all its fullness.

Go in Great Peace

My daughter, tell souls that I am giving them My mercy as a defense. I Myself am fighting for them and am bearing the just anger of My Father (*Diary*, 1516).

April 20, [1938]. Departure for Pradnik. I was very worried that I would be put in bed in a ward and be exposed to all sorts of things. If it were to be for only a week or two … but it is for such a long time, two months or perhaps more. In the evening, I went in for a long talk with the Lord Jesus. When I saw the Lord Jesus, I poured out my whole heart before Him, all my troubles, fears, and apprehensions. Jesus lovingly listened to me and then said, **Be at peace, My child, I am with you. Go in great peace. All is ready; I have ordered, in My own special way, a private room to be prepared for you.** Reassured and overwhelmed with gratitude, I went to bed (*Diary*, 1674).

My Prayer Response:

Thank You, Lord Jesus, for teaching us to trust in Your mercy. Your mercy is our defense in battle and our peace in anxiety.

Novena before the Feast of Mercy

March 22 – 30

In His revelations to St. Faustina, Jesus describes a novena that He wants her to make before the Feast of Mercy. He commands the great Apostle of Divine Mercy to keep it and describes its powerful purpose this way:

> Jesus is commanding me to make a novena before the Feast of Mercy, and today I am to begin it for the conversion of the whole world and for the recognition of The Divine Mercy … **so that every soul will praise My goodness. I desire trust from My creatures. Encourage souls to place great trust in My fathomless mercy. Let the weak, sinful soul have no fear to approach Me, for even if it had more sins than there are grains of sand in the world, all would be drowned in the immeasurable depths of My mercy** (*Diary,* 1059).

This prayer is essentially a novena of Divine Mercy Chaplets for souls, which begins on Good Friday and ends on the Saturday before Divine Mercy Sunday. It carries this amazing promise from the Lord: **By this novena, I will grant every possible grace to souls** (*Diary,* 796).

Jesus explained the novena in this way to St. Faustina and gave her — as we shall see — a different group of souls to pray for on each of the nine days:

> **I desire that during these nine days you bring souls to the fountain of My mercy,**

that they may draw from there strength and refreshment and whatever grace they need in the hardships of life, and especially at the hour of death.

On each day you will bring to My Heart a different group of souls, and you will immerse them in this ocean of My mercy, and I will bring all these souls into the house of My Father. You will do this in this life and in the next. I will deny nothing to any soul whom you will bring to the fount of My mercy. On each day you will beg My Father, on the strength of My bitter Passion, for graces for these souls (*Diary*, 1209).

As apostles of Divine Mercy, we can join St. Faustina in praying this wonderful novena for souls. Millions of faithful souls do just that before Divine Mercy Sunday each year. Some pray the novena frequently, even perpetually, for souls. At the National Shrine of The Divine Mercy in Stockbridge, Massachusetts, the Marians of the Immaculate Conception pray it perpetually each day at 3 p.m., the Hour of Great Mercy.

A Note to the Reader: As you go through the novena in the pages that follow, there are footnotes to some of the days. You can find them at the back of this book.

First Day

Today bring to Me ALL MANKIND, ESPECIALLY ALL SINNERS, and immerse them in the ocean of My mercy. In this way you will console Me in the bitter grief into which the loss of souls plunges Me (*Diary,* 1210).

My Prayer Response with St. Faustina:

Most Merciful Jesus, whose very nature it is to have compassion on us and to forgive us, do not look upon our sins but upon our trust which we place in Your infinite goodness. Receive us all into the abode of Your Most Compassionate Heart, and never let us escape from It. We beg this of You by Your love which unites You to the Father and the Holy Spirit (*Diary,* 1211).

Second Day

Today bring to Me THE SOULS OF PRIESTS AND RELIGIOUS,[1] and immerse them in My unfathomable mercy. It was they who gave Me strength to endure My bitter Passion. Through them, as through channels, My mercy flows out upon mankind (*Diary*, 1212).

My Prayer Response with St. Faustina:

Most Merciful Jesus, from whom comes all that is good, increase Your grace in men and women consecrated to Your service, that they may perform worthy works of mercy; and that all who see them may glorify the Father of Mercy who is in heaven (*Diary*, 1213).

Third Day

Today bring to Me ALL DEVOUT AND FAITHFUL SOULS, and immerse them in the ocean of My mercy. These souls brought Me consolation on the Way of the Cross. They were that drop of consolation in the midst of an ocean of bitterness (*Diary*, 1214).

My Prayer Response with St. Faustina:

Most Merciful Jesus, from the treasury of Your mercy, You impart Your graces in great abundance to each and all. Receive us into the abode of Your Most Compassionate Heart and never let us escape from It. We beg this grace of You by that most wondrous love for the heavenly Father with which Your Heart burns so fiercely (*Diary*, 1215).

Fourth Day

Today bring to Me THOSE WHO DO NOT BELIEVE IN GOD AND THOSE WHO DO NOT YET KNOW ME.[2] I was thinking also of them during My bitter Passion, and their future zeal comforted My Heart. Immerse them in the ocean of My mercy (*Diary*, 1216).

My Prayer Response with St. Faustina:

Most compassionate Jesus, You are the Light of the whole world. Receive into the abode of Your Most Compassionate Heart the souls of those who do not believe in God and of those who as yet do not know You. Let the rays of Your grace enlighten them that they, too, together with us, may extol Your wonderful mercy; and do not let them escape from the abode which is Your Most Compassionate Heart (*Diary*, 1217).

Fifth Day

Today bring to Me THE SOULS OF THOSE WHO HAVE SEPARATED THEMSELVES FROM MY CHURCH,[3] and immerse them in the ocean of My mercy. During My bitter Passion they tore at My Body and Heart, that is, My Church. As they return to unity with the Church, My wounds heal and in this way they alleviate My Passion (*Diary,* 1218).

My Prayer Response with St. Faustina:

Most Merciful Jesus, Goodness Itself, You do not refuse light to those who seek it of You. Receive into the abode of Your Most Compassionate Heart the souls of those who have separated themselves from Your Church. Draw them by Your light into the unity of the Church, and do not let them escape from the abode of Your Most Compassionate Heart; but bring it about that they, too, come to glorify the generosity of Your mercy (*Diary,* 1219).

Sixth Day

Today bring to Me THE MEEK AND HUMBLE SOULS AND THE SOULS OF LITTLE CHILDREN, and immerse them in My mercy. These souls most closely resemble My Heart. They strengthened Me during My bitter agony. I saw them as earthly Angels, who will keep vigil at My altars. I pour out upon them whole torrents of grace. Only the humble soul is capable of receiving My grace. I favor humble souls with My confidence (*Diary*, 1220).

My Prayer Response with St. Faustina:

Most Merciful Jesus, You Yourself have said, "Learn from Me for I am meek and humble of heart." Receive into the abode of Your Most Compassionate Heart all meek and humble souls and the souls of little children. These souls send all heaven into ecstasy and they are the heavenly Father's favorites. They are a sweet-smelling bouquet before the throne of God; God Himself takes delight in their fragrance. These souls have a permanent abode in Your Most Compassionate Heart, O Jesus, and they unceasingly sing out a hymn of love and mercy (*Diary*, 1221).

Seventh Day

Today bring to Me THE SOULS WHO ESPECIALLY VENERATE AND GLORIFY MY MERCY,[4] and immerse them in My mercy. These souls sorrowed most over My Passion and entered most deeply into My spirit. They are living images of My Compassionate Heart. These souls will shine with a special brightness in the next life. Not one of them will go into the fire of hell. I shall particularly defend each one of them at the hour of death (*Diary,* 1224).

My Prayer Response with St. Faustina:

Most Merciful Jesus, whose Heart is Love Itself, receive into the abode of Your Most Compassionate Heart the souls of those who particularly extol and venerate the greatness of Your mercy. These souls are mighty with the very power of God Himself. In the midst of all afflictions and adversities they go forward, confident of Your mercy. These souls are united to Jesus and carry all mankind on their shoulders. These souls will not be judged severely, but Your mercy will embrace them as they depart from this life (*Diary,* 1225).

Eighth Day

Today bring to Me THE SOULS WHO ARE DETAINED IN PURGATORY, and immerse them in the abyss of My mercy. Let the torrents of My Blood cool down their scorching flames. All these souls are greatly loved by Me. They are making retribution to My justice. It is in your power to bring them relief. Draw all the indulgences from the treasury of My Church and offer them on their behalf. Oh, if you only knew the torments they suffer, you would continually offer for them the alms of the spirit and pay off their debt to My justice (*Diary,* 1226).

My Prayer Response with St. Faustina:

Most Merciful Jesus, You Yourself have said that You desire mercy; so I bring into the abode of Your Most Compassionate Heart the souls in Purgatory, souls who are very dear to You, and yet, who must make retribution to Your justice. May the streams of Blood and Water which gushed forth from Your Heart put out the flames of Purgatory, that there, too, the power of Your mercy may be praised (*Diary,* 1227).

Ninth Day

Today bring to Me SOULS WHO HAVE BECOME LUKEWARM,[5] and immerse them in the abyss of My mercy. These souls wound My Heart most painfully. My soul suffered the most dreadful loathing in the Garden of Olives because of lukewarm souls. They were the reason I cried out: "Father, take this cup away from Me, if it be Your will." For them, the last hope of salvation is to flee to My mercy (*Diary,* 1228).

My Prayer Response with St. Faustina:

Most compassionate Jesus, You are Compassion Itself. I bring lukewarm souls into the abode of Your Most Compassionate Heart. In this fire of Your pure love, let these tepid souls, who, like corpses, filled You with such deep loathing, be once again set aflame. O Most Compassionate Jesus, exercise the omnipotence of Your mercy and draw them into the very ardor of Your love, and bestow upon them the gift of holy love, for nothing is beyond Your power (*Diary,* 1229).

The Feast of Mercy

March 31 – April 10

The Sunday after Easter is now called Divine Mercy Sunday by the declaration of Pope John Paul II. He established it as a universal feast day in the Church on the day that he canonized St. Faustina, the great Apostle of Divine Mercy. It is significant that the date was April 30, 2000, which was Divine Mercy Sunday that year.

Divine Mercy Sunday is the celebration of the Feast of Mercy that our Lord asked of St. Faustina. This Feast of Mercy is a focal point that summarizes The Divine Mercy message and devotion. It fulfills an important desire of His Heart that the Lord made known to St. Faustina — to literally loose the floodgates of His mercy on this day.

Jesus promises unfathomable graces on this day to souls that will go to confession beforehand and then receive Him worthily in Holy Communion on the Feast of Mercy (see *Diary*, 699.) Under certain conditions, the Church has also granted a plenary indulgence to the faithful who celebrate Divine Mercy Sunday.

I believe that the Church's celebration of Divine Mercy Sunday shows that The Divine Mercy message and devotion is God's answer to the crises in the Church and in our troubled world. The words of our Lord to St. Faustina, repeatedly quoted by Pope John Paul II, confirm God's answer: **Mankind will not have peace until it turns with trust to My mercy** (*Diary*, 300; also see 699 and 1074).

Our Lord spoke directly to St. Faustina about the significance of Divine Mercy Sunday:

> **Souls perish in spite of My bitter Passion. *I am giving them the last hope of salvation; that is, the Feast of My Mercy.* If they will not adore My mercy, they will perish for all eternity** (*Diary*, 965, emphasis added).

In a similar vein, Pope John Paul II wrote in his last book, *Memory and Identity*, that "the limit imposed upon evil … is ultimately Divine Mercy" (p. 55). Cardinal Joseph Ratzinger, now Pope Benedict XVI, quoted this powerful statement about Divine Mercy at the funeral of Pope John Paul II.

Let us do everything we can in light of all this to prepare well each year to celebrate Divine Mercy Sunday. And let's encourage every person in our parishes to join us in celebrating the Feast of Mercy.

Solemnly Bless This Image

When I told this to my confessor, I received this for a reply: "That refers to your soul." He told me, "Certainly, paint God's image in your soul." When I came out of the confessional, I again heard words such as these: **My image already is in your soul. I desire that there be a Feast of Mercy. I want this image, which you will paint with a brush, to be solemnly blessed on the first Sunday after Easter; that Sunday is to be the Feast of Mercy** (*Diary*, 49).

My Prayer Response:

Thank You, Jesus, that Your image as The Divine Mercy, radiating Your mercy and blessing us, has been painted and is available for our veneration. Thank You that the Feast of Mercy is now available to the whole Church as a special moment of grace. With deep trust in You, may I venerate Your image on the Feast of Mercy.

Approach the Fount of Life

I desire that the first Sunday after Easter be the Feast of Mercy (*Diary*, 299).

Ask of my faithful servant [Father Sopocko] **that, on this day, he tell the whole world of My great mercy; that whoever approaches the Fount of Life on this day will be granted complete remission of sins and punishment. Mankind will not have peace until it turns with trust to My mercy** (*Diary*, 300).

My Prayer Response:

"Mankind so needs to understand and accept Divine Mercy" (John Paul II, posthumous Divine Mercy Sunday message, April 3, 2005). Lord Jesus, help us to believe in the promise You made about Mercy Sunday and turn to Your mercy with trust.

May Every Soul Know

I am very surprised that You bid me to talk about this Feast of Mercy, for they tell me that there is already such a feast and so why should I talk about it? And Jesus said to me, **And who knows anything about this feast? No one! Even those who should be proclaiming My mercy and teaching people about it often do not know about it themselves. That is why I want the image to be solemnly blessed on the first Sunday after Easter, and I want it to be venerated publicly so that every soul may know about it** (*Diary*, 341).

My Prayer Response:

Lord Jesus, may the Feast of Mercy be explained and understood and celebrated, so every soul may know about it. May The Feast of Mercy be a great evangelistic tool in reaching the whole world with Your mercy!

The First Feast of Mercy

Low Sunday; that is, the Feast of The Divine Mercy, the conclusion of the Jubilee of Redemption. When we went to take part in the celebrations, my heart leapt with joy that the two solemnities were so closely united. I asked God for mercy on the souls of sinners. Toward the end of the service, when the priest took the Blessed Sacrament to bless the people, I saw the Lord Jesus as He is represented in the image. The Lord gave His blessing, and the rays extended over the whole world. … I heard a voice, **This Feast emerged from the very depths of My mercy, and it is confirmed in the vast depths of My tender mercies. Every soul believing and trusting in My mercy will obtain it** (*Diary*, 420).

My Prayer Response:

Thank you, St. Faustina, for your description of the first celebration of the Feast of Mercy, at the Shrine of Our Lady, Mother of Mercy in Vilnius (Shrine of Ostra Brama [The Dawn Gate]). What a marvel of God's timing that it was also the world's celebration of the 1,933rd anniversary of our redemption!

A Shelter for All Souls

On one occasion, I heard these words: **My daughter, tell the whole world about My inconceivable mercy. I desire that the Feast of Mercy be a refuge and shelter for all souls, and especially for poor sinners. On that day the very depths of My tender mercy are open. I pour out a whole ocean of graces upon those souls who approach the Fount of My Mercy. The soul that will go to Confession and receive Holy Communion shall obtain complete forgiveness of sins and punishment** (*Diary*, 699).

My Prayer Response:

Lord Jesus, Thank You for the Feast of Mercy as a shelter for all souls, especially for poor sinners. May I prepare with confident faith to receive the graces You promise for us on that day. I want to plunge into the ocean of Your graces.

The Divine Floodgates

On that day all the divine floodgates through which graces flow are opened. Let no soul fear to draw near to Me, even though its sins be as scarlet. My mercy is so great that no mind, be it of man or of angel, will be able to fathom it throughout all eternity (*Diary*, 699).

My Prayer Response:

Lord, what a promise! All the divine floodgates are open to pour out Your graces upon us. Help us to desire, to ask for, and to receive with thanksgiving Your mercy that You pour out upon us. May we share the good news of these graces with our brothers and sisters.

The Very Depths of Tenderness

Everything that exists has come forth from the very depths of My most tender mercy. Every soul in its relation to Me will contemplate My love and mercy throughout eternity. The Feast of Mercy emerged from My very depths of tenderness. It is My desire that it be solemnly celebrated on the first Sunday after Easter. Mankind will not have peace until it turns to the Fount of My Mercy (*Diary*, 699).

My Prayer Response:

Thank You, Jesus, for the Feast of Mercy that comes from the very depths of Your tenderness. May mankind find peace by turning to this fount of Your mercy.

Adore My Mercy

Jesus looked at me and said, **Souls perish in spite of My bitter Passion. I am giving them the last hope of salvation; that is, the Feast of My Mercy. If they will not adore My mercy, they will perish for all eternity. Secretary of My mercy, write, tell souls about this great mercy of Mine, because the awful day, the day of My justice, is near** (*Diary,* 965).

My Prayer Response:

Thank You, Jesus, for Your stern warning about Your gift of the Feast of Mercy. By a sovereign act of Your Mercy, draw mankind to adore Your great mercy — lest they perish for all eternity. Have mercy, O Lord!

Complete Pardon

I want to grant a complete pardon to the souls that will go to Confession and receive Holy Communion on the Feast of My mercy. Then He said to me, **My daughter, fear nothing. I am always with you, even if it seems to you that I am not. Your humility draws Me down from My lofty throne, and I unite Myself closely with you** (*Diary*, 1109).

My Prayer Response:

Lord Jesus, draw all souls, especially poor sinners, to turn to Your mercy on the Feast of Mercy and receive complete pardon! Help us to fear nothing and place our trust in You.

Hastening the Feast of Mercy

For the sake of your ardent desires, I am hastening the Feast of Mercy. My spirit burst into such a powerful flame of love that it seemed to me that I was totally dissolved in God (*Diary*, 1082).

My Prayer Response:

Praised be the Lord Jesus Christ! The promise of Jesus in hastening the Feast of Mercy was fulfilled by Pope John Paul II on the day of the canonization of St. Faustina, which was on Divine Mercy Sunday, April 30, 2000. Lord Jesus, bless Pope John Paul II, who that day declared the Second Sunday of Easter as Divine Mercy Sunday! Bless Him by hastening his canonization.

Consolation for Souls

Say, My daughter, that the Feast of My Mercy has issued forth from My very depths for the consolation of the whole world (*Diary*, 1517).

My Prayer Response:

Thank You, Lord Jesus, that the Feast of Mercy is now available. May the feast be celebrated, so souls in need would receive consolation. Lord Jesus, Son of the Living God, have mercy on us and on the whole world!

The Chaplet of Mercy

April 11 – 20

Jesus taught St. Faustina a powerful intercessory prayer that is Eucharistic. It is known as the Chaplet of Divine Mercy. This chaplet is now prayed by millions the world over at 3 p.m., the Hour of Great Mercy, although it can be prayed at any time. In this prayer, we offer God the Father **the Body and Blood, Soul and Divinity of Your dearly beloved Son, Our Lord Jesus Christ, in atonement for our sins and those of the whole world** (*Diary*, 476).

The power of the Chaplet of Divine Mercy was taught by Jesus and demonstrated by St. Faustina's praying it in a variety of situations, especially at the bedside of the dying. One sign of its efficacy is the way so many Divine Mercy devotees have reported that loved ones have died a peaceful death after they prayed it at the bedside of the dying person.

Millions of Catholics have seen The Divine Mercy Chaplet prayed at the three o'clock hour on EWTN's global Catholic network. Many more have read about this prayer in booklets or viewed it on DVD through publications from Marian Press, which is the publishing house of the Marians of the Immaculate Conception. The Chaplet of Divine Mercy is prayed every day at the National Shrine of The Divine Mercy, which the Marians administer in Stockbridge, Massachusetts.

It's instructive that Jesus' revelation of this prayer began with a vision in which St. Faustina saw an angel about to carry out the divine wrath against a certain place that could not be named:

> In the evening when I was in my cell, I saw an Angel, the executor of divine wrath. ... I began to implore the Angel to hold off for a few moments, and the world would do penance. But my plea was a mere nothing in the face of the divine anger. Just then I saw the Most Holy Trinity. The greatness of Its majesty pierced me deeply, and I did not dare to repeat my entreaties. At that very moment I felt in my soul the power of Jesus' grace, which dwells in my soul. When I became conscious of this grace, I was instantly snatched up before the Throne of God. Oh, how great is our Lord and God and how incomprehensible His Holiness! I will make no attempt to describe this greatness, because before long we shall all see Him as He is. I found myself pleading with God for the world with words I heard interiorly.
>
> As I was praying in this manner, I saw the Angel's helplessness: he could not carry out the just punishment which was rightly due for sins. Never before had I prayed with such inner power as I did then (*Diary*, 474).

The entries that immediately follow provide the text of The Divine Mercy Chaplet and instructions on how to pray it. I invite you to recite this prayer for mercy every day, especially at 3 p.m. and at the bedside of anyone you know who is dying.

Offering the Sacrifice

The words with which I entreated God are these: **Eternal Father, I offer You the Body and Blood, Soul and Divinity of Your dearly beloved Son, Our Lord Jesus Christ for our sins and those of the whole world; for the sake of His sorrowful Passion, have mercy on us** (*Diary,* 475).

The next morning, when I entered chapel, I heard these words interiorly: **Every time you enter the chapel, immediately recite the prayer which I taught you yesterday** (*Diary,* 476).

My Prayer Response:

Thank You, Lord, for the prayer of the Chaplet of Mercy. It is "living the Mass," offering the sacrifice of Your Body and Blood, Soul and Divinity to the Father — for mercy on the whole world.

A Powerful Prayer Weapon

When I had said the prayer, in my soul I heard these words: **This prayer will serve to appease My wrath. You will recite it for nine days, on the beads of the rosary, in the following manner: First of all, you will say one OUR FATHER and HAIL MARY and the I BELIEVE IN GOD. Then on the OUR FATHER beads you will say the following words: "Eternal Father, I offer You the Body and Blood, Soul and Divinity of Your dearly beloved Son, Our Lord Jesus Christ, in atonement for our sins and those of the whole world." On the HAIL MARY beads you will say the following words: "For the sake of His sorrowful Passion have mercy on us and on the whole world." In conclusion, three times you will recite these words: "Holy God, Holy Mighty One, Holy Immortal One, have mercy on us and on the whole world"** *(Diary,* 476).

My Prayer Response:

Thank You, Jesus, for the powerful prayer weapon You have given us. Help us to use it regularly for mercy not only for ourselves but for the whole world! Thank You for the global consciousness You give us of the world's need of Your mercy.

Say Unceasingly the Chaplet

Once, as I was going down the hall to the kitchen, I heard these words in my soul: **Say unceasingly the chaplet that I have taught you. Whoever will recite it will receive great mercy at the hour of death. Priests will recommend it to sinners as their last hope of salvation. Even if there were a sinner most hardened, if he were to recite this chaplet only once, he would receive grace from My infinite mercy. I desire that the whole world know My infinite mercy. I desire to grant unimaginable graces to those souls who trust in My mercy** (*Diary*, 687).

My Prayer Response:

Lord Jesus, make me more aware of the power of the mercy chaplet as a prayer for Your infinite mercy for sinners, for the dying, and for the whole world. May You inspire me to pray it unceasingly.

A Prayer for the Dying

The Lord said to me today: **Go to the Superior and tell her that I want all the sisters and wards to say the chaplet which I have taught you. They are to say it for nine days in the chapel in order to appease My Father and to entreat God's mercy for Poland** (*Diary*, 714).

The following afternoon, when I entered the ward, I saw someone dying, and learned that the agony had started during the night. When I verified it — it had been at the time when I had been asked for prayer. And just then, I heard a voice in my soul: **Say the chaplet which I taught you.** I ran to fetch my rosary and knelt down by the dying person and, with all the ardor of my soul, I began to say the chaplet. Suddenly the dying person opened her eyes and looked at me; I had not managed to finish the entire chaplet when she died, with extraordinary peace (*Diary*, 810).

My Prayer Response:

Thank You, Jesus, for this powerful prayer for the dying. I have seen the effect of praying the Chaplet of Divine Mercy for my dying sister. Peace at her death filled the room!

At the Hour of Death

When I entered my solitude, I heard these words: **At the hour of their death, I defend as My own glory every soul that will say this chaplet; or when others say it for a dying person, the pardon is the same. When this chaplet is said by the bedside of a dying person, God's anger is placated, unfathomable mercy envelops the soul, and the very depths of My tender mercy are moved for the sake of the sorrowful Passion of My Son** (*Diary,* 811).

My Prayer Response:

Lord Jesus, thank You for the promises You and Your Father made about praying the Chaplet of Divine Mercy for the dying. Help us to make use of it for dying family members and friends.

Bringing Humankind Closer to Me

While I was saying the chaplet, I heard a voice which said, **Oh, what great graces I will grant to souls who say this chaplet; the very depths of My tender mercy are stirred for the sake of those who say the chaplet** (*Diary,* 848).

Jesus listened to these outpourings of my heart with gravity and interest, as if He had known nothing about them, and this seemed to make it easier for me to talk. And the Lord said to me, **My daughter, those words of your heart are pleasing to Me, and by saying the chaplet you are bringing humankind closer to Me.** After these words, I found myself alone, but the presence of God is always in my soul (*Diary,* 929).

My Prayer Response:

Lord Jesus, increase my trust in You and in Your promises of great graces for saying the Chaplet of Divine Mercy. May my prayer be pleasing to You and bring souls closer to You.

Encourage Souls to Say the Chaplet

My daughter, encourage souls to say the chaplet which I have given to you. It pleases Me to grant everything they ask of Me by saying the chaplet. When hardened sinners say it, I will fill their souls with peace, and the hour of their death will be a happy one.

Write that when they say this chaplet in the presence of the dying, I will stand between My Father and the dying person, not as the just Judge but as the merciful Savior (*Diary,* 1541).

My Prayer Response:

Lord Jesus, help me not only to please You by praying the Chaplet of Divine Mercy but also help me to encourage others to pray it. May many more souls avail themselves of this powerful intercessory prayer, especially in praying for the dying.

The Powers of Darkness Flee

When I entered the chapel for a moment, the Lord said to me, **My daughter, help Me to save a certain dying sinner. Say the chaplet that I have taught you for him.** When I began to say the chaplet, I saw the man dying in the midst of terrible torment and struggle. His Guardian Angel was defending him, but he was, as it were, powerless against the enormity of the soul's misery. A multitude of devils was waiting for the soul. But while I was saying the chaplet, I saw Jesus just as He is depicted in the image. The rays which issued from Jesus' Heart enveloped the sick man, and the powers of darkness fled in panic. The sick man peacefully breathed his last. When I came to myself, I understood how very important the chaplet was for the dying. It appeases the anger of God (*Diary,* 1565).

My Prayer Response:

Lord, thank You for the power of The Divine Mercy Chaplet for the dying, especially to defend them against the powers of darkness. When I am dying, Lord, defend me against the Evil One.

In a Great Storm

Today I was awakened by a great storm. The wind was raging, and it was raining in torrents, thunderbolts striking again and again. I began to pray that the storm would do no harm, when I heard the words: **Say the chaplet I have taught you, and the storm will cease.** I began immediately to say the chaplet and hadn't even finished it when the storm suddenly ceased, and I heard the words: **Through the chaplet you will obtain everything, if what you ask for is compatible with My will** (*Diary,* 1731).

My Prayer Response:

Thank You, Jesus, for teaching us to use the Chaplet of Divine Mercy for a variety of needs. What amazing promises You have made about our praying it.

Peace to the Tormented Soul

Today, the Lord came to me and said, **My daughter, help Me to save souls. You will go to a dying sinner, and you will continue to recite the chaplet, and in this way you will obtain for him trust in My mercy, for he is already in despair** (*Diary*, 1797).

Suddenly, I found myself in a strange cottage where an elderly man was dying amidst great torments. All about the bed was a multitude of demons and the family, who were crying. When I began to pray, the spirits of darkness fled, with hissing and threats directed at me. The soul became calm and, filled with trust, rested in the Lord.

At the same moment, I found myself again in my own room. How this happens … I do not know (*Diary*, 1798).

My Prayer Response:

Thank You, Jesus, for the gift of trust for the dying as we pray the Chaplet of Divine Mercy. You dispel a multitude of demons and bring peace to the tormented soul.

Proclaim My Mercy

April 21 – May 2

Jesus exhorts St. Faustina, **Tell the world about My mercy and My love** (*Diary,* 1074). This exhortation was foundational to the saint's call to be the Lord's great Apostle of Mercy by proclaiming His mercy to all mankind. As Jesus also tells her, **Apostle of My mercy, proclaim to the whole world My unfathomable mercy** (*Diary,* 1142).

The good news is that this is not only an exhortation and command to St. Faustina — it is also an exhortation and command to you and me to become apostles of mercy ourselves!

Look around you. The whole world is in desperate need of God's mercy. Tell anyone who will listen about God's mercy. Do whatever you can to spread the message of Divine Mercy by personal witness. Distribute pamphlets on Divine Mercy. Pray The Divine Mercy Chaplet for God's mercy on the whole world now, while it is still the time for mercy.

As you set about this important task and read the following entries, consider the promise of Jesus: **Souls who spread the honor of My mercy I shield through their entire lives as a tender mother her infant, and at the hour of death I will not be a Judge for them, but the Merciful Savior** (*Diary,* 1075).

In responding to this call, you will be in good company with St. Faustina and Pope John Paul II, who tirelessly proclaimed God's mercy as the Great Mercy Pope. In fact, Pope Benedict XVI said on the third anniversary of this great Pope's death, "Like Sr. Faustina, John Paul II in his turn made himself an apostle of Divine Mercy" (Homily, April 2, 2008). What an inspiration for us!

My Inconceivable Mercy

Jesus said to me with kindness, **My daughter, speak to priests about this inconceivable mercy of Mine. The flames of mercy are burning Me — clamoring to be spent; I want to keep pouring them out upon souls; souls just don't want to believe in My goodness** (*Diary,* 177).

My Prayer response:

Lord Jesus, give priests a special grace to hear the word of Your inconceivable mercy and to proclaim it to people in need. May distrustful souls come to believe in Your goodness as they hear it proclaimed.

My Greatest Attribute

Proclaim that mercy is the greatest attribute of God. All the works of My hands are crowned with mercy (*Diary*, 301).

Everything that you say about My goodness is true; language has no adequate expression to extol My goodness (*Diary*, 359).

My Prayer Response:

Lord Jesus, help me to express and articulate clearly Your goodness. How can I speak of Your greatest attribute of mercy without Your grace? Fill me then, so I can proclaim Your mercy.

My Own Glory

But God has promised a great grace especially to you [Father Sopocko] and to all those … **who will proclaim My great mercy. I shall protect them Myself at the hour of death, as My own glory. And even if the sins of souls were as dark as night, when the sinner turns to My mercy, he gives Me the greatest praise and is the glory of My Passion. When a soul extols My goodness, Satan trembles before it and flees to the very bottom of hell** (*Diary*, 378).

My Prayer Response:

Lord Jesus, I claim Your promise for myself and for all apostles of Divine Mercy: May we be protected as Your own glory at the hour of death, and may Satan tremble and flee to the very bottom of hell.

Claiming Your Promise

During one of the adorations, Jesus promised me that: **With souls that have recourse to My mercy and with those that glorify and proclaim My great mercy to others, I will deal according to My infinite mercy at the hour of their death** (*Diary,* 379).

My Prayer Response:

Jesus, You promised to deal according to Your mercy with all who have recourse to Your mercy — those who glorify it and those who proclaim Your mercy to others. I claim Your promise for all those who are devoted to Your Divine Mercy!

The Last Hope of Salvation

I heard a voice in my soul: **These words are for you. Do all you possibly can for this work of My mercy. I desire that My mercy be worshiped, and I am giving mankind the last hope of salvation; that is, recourse to My mercy. My Heart rejoices in this feast.** After these words, I understood that nothing can dispense me from the obligation which the Lord demands from me (*Diary*, 998).

My Prayer Response:

Lord Jesus, help me and all souls to *worship* Your mercy and to have recourse to Your mercy as the last hope of salvation for mankind.

Rouse Others to Love Me

I heard a voice within my soul. **I am very pleased that you had not been talking with Me, but were making My goodness known to souls and rousing them to love Me** (*Diary,* 404).

Tell the world about My mercy and My love (*Diary,* 1074).

My Prayer Response:

Dear Jesus, teach me and all apostles of Divine Mercy to tell the world about Your mercy and love — and rouse them to love You! May the whole world come to know of Your mercy.

Special Devotion to My Mercy

The flames of mercy are burning Me. I desire to pour them out upon human souls. Oh, what pain they cause Me when they do not want to accept them!

My daughter, do whatever is within your power to spread devotion to My mercy. I will make up for what you lack. Tell aching mankind to snuggle close to My merciful Heart, and I will fill it with peace (*Diary,* 1074).

My Prayer Response:

Lord Jesus, help me and all apostles of Divine Mercy to tell aching mankind of Your great desire to pour out Your mercy upon human souls and for them to snuggle close to Your merciful Heart.

Spread the Honor of My Mercy

Souls who spread the honor of My mercy I shield through their entire lives as a tender mother her infant, and at the hour of death I will not be a Judge for them, but the Merciful Savior. At that last hour, a soul has nothing with which to defend itself except My mercy. Happy is the soul that during its lifetime immersed itself in the Fountain of Mercy, because justice will have no hold on it (*Diary,* 1075).

My Prayer Response:

O my Jesus, immerse me and all promoters of Divine Mercy in the Fountain of Your mercy, the source of joy during our lifetime. Shield us through our entire lives as a tender mother does her infant.

Do Not Be Discouraged

I heard a voice: **Apostle of My mercy, proclaim to the whole world My unfathomable mercy. Do not be discouraged by the difficulties you encounter in proclaiming My mercy. These difficulties that affect you so painfully are needed for your sanctification and evidence that this work is Mine** (*Diary,* 1142).

My Prayer Response:

Lord Jesus, do not let us apostles of Divine Mercy be discouraged by the difficulties we encounter, but may we rejoice in them because they are needed for our sanctification — it is all Your work. All for the glory of Your name, Merciful Savior.

My Mercy as a Defense

My daughter, tell souls that I am giving them My mercy as a defense. I Myself am fighting for them and am bearing the just anger of My Father (*Diary,* 1516).

Today before Holy Communion, the Lord said to me, **My daughter, today talk openly to the superior** [Mother Irene] **about My mercy because, of all the superiors, she has taken the greatest part in proclaiming My mercy** (*Diary,* 1519).

My Prayer Response:

Thank You, Jesus, that You give Your mercy as our defense in the battle of life — and that You Yourself are fighting for us. Help me to talk openly of Your mercy to others, not giving into discouragement.

Refresh This Heart of Mine

The Lord said to me, **My daughter, do not tire of proclaiming My mercy. In this way you will refresh this Heart of Mine, which burns with a flame of pity for sinners. Tell My priests that hardened sinners will repent on hearing their words when they speak about My unfathomable mercy, about the compassion I have for them in My Heart. To priests who proclaim and extol My mercy, I will give wondrous power; I will anoint their words and touch the hearts of those to whom they will speak** (*Diary*, 1521).

My Prayer Response:

Lord Jesus, I want to refresh Your Heart by unfailingly proclaiming Your mercy. Thank You for empowering Your priests with anointed words of mercy that touch the hearts of the people. Remind me, Lord, to pray for priests that they would not stint in proclaiming Your mercy.

No Terror at the Hour of Death

January 28, 1938. Today the Lord said to me, **My daughter, write down these words: All those souls who will glorify My mercy and spread its worship, encouraging others to trust in My mercy, will not experience terror at the hour of death. My mercy will shield them in that final battle ...** (*Diary*, 1540).

My Prayer Response:

Lord Jesus, thank You for Your repeated promise to those who glorify Your mercy and encourage others to trust in Your mercy — that You will shield them with Your mercy in the final battle. I pray that all those who are apostles of Divine Mercy would claim this powerful promise.

The Three O'clock Hour of Mercy

May 3 – 6

Jesus encouraged St. Faustina to pray at 3 p.m. every day, remembering His Passion and pleading mercy for sinners. Among those in The Divine Mercy movement, this has become known as the Hour of Great Mercy. Many devotees recite the Chaplet of Divine Mercy during this hour.

Jesus instructed St. Faustina, **At three o'clock, implore My mercy, especially for sinners; and, if only for a brief moment, immerse yourself in My Passion, particularly in My abandonment at the moment of agony** (*Diary*, 1320). He also encouraged her, **Try your best to make the Stations of the Cross in this hour, provided that your duties permit it** (*Diary*, 1572).

Given our own circumstances, we can discern with the Holy Spirit's help what is possible for us to do at the Hour of Great Mercy every day. It may be uniting our heart to the Lord in His Passion for a brief moment. It may mean praying The Divine Mercy Chaplet or making the Stations of the Cross. It's also an ideal time to make a daily Holy Hour before our Lord in the Blessed Sacrament.

May these passages from the *Diary* inspire you to observe the Hour of Great Mercy, the hour Jesus died for you on the cross.

You Are My Solace

At three o'clock, I prayed prostrate, in the form of a cross, for the whole world. Jesus' mortal life was coming to an end. I heard His seven words; then He looked at me and said, **Beloved daughter of My Heart, you are My solace amidst terrible torments** (*Diary*, 1058).

My Prayer Response with St. Faustina:

You expired, Jesus, but the source of life gushed forth for souls, and the ocean of mercy opened up for the whole world. O Fount of Life, unfathomable Divine Mercy, envelop the whole world and empty Yourself out upon us (*Diary*, 1319).

Immerse Yourself in My Passion

At three o'clock, implore My mercy, especially for sinners; and, if only for a brief moment, immerse yourself in My Passion, particularly in My abandonment at the moment of agony. This is the hour of great mercy for the whole world. I will allow you to enter into My mortal sorrow. In this hour, I will refuse nothing to the soul that makes a request of Me in virtue of My Passion ... (*Diary*, 1320).

My Prayer Response:

Lord Jesus, help me to take good advantage of the Hour of Great Mercy and remember Your passion. I desire to immerse myself in Your Passion. I beg for Your mercy upon the whole world, especially sinners.

At That Moment, Mercy Was Opened Wide

I remind you, My daughter, that as often as you hear the clock strike the third hour, immerse yourself completely in My mercy, adoring and glorifying it; invoke its omnipotence for the whole world, and particularly for poor sinners; for at that moment mercy was opened wide for every soul. In this hour you can obtain everything for yourself and for others for the asking; it was the hour of grace for the whole world — mercy triumphed over justice (*Diary*, 1572).

My Prayer Response:

Lord Jesus, remind me to immerse myself in the ocean of Your mercy at the three o'clock hour, adoring and glorifying Your great mercy and invoking Your mercy on the whole world so very much in need of mercy. May I and all apostles of Divine Mercy "get the three o'clock habit"!

Ways to Pray at Three O'clock

My daughter, try your best to make the Stations of the Cross in this hour, provided that your duties permit it; and if you are not able to make the Stations of the Cross, then at least step into the chapel for a moment and adore, in the Blessed Sacrament, My Heart, which is full of mercy; and should you be unable to step into the chapel, immerse yourself in prayer there where you happen to be, if only for a very brief instant. I claim veneration for My mercy from every creature, but above all from you, since it is to you that I have given the most profound understanding of this mystery (*Diary,* 1572).

My Prayer Response:

Lord Jesus, You so desire that we take advantage of the Hour of Great Mercy that You offer us a variety of ways to venerate Your mercy. Help us to draw down all the available graces for a world in desperate need of Your mercy.

Meditate upon My Passion

May 7 – 19

The call to meditate upon the Passion of our Lord and Savior Jesus Christ fits in perfectly with praying the Chaplet of Divine Mercy and observing the Hour of Great Mercy at 3 p.m. In The Divine Mercy Chaplet, we plead before the Eternal Father: **For the sake of His sorrowful Passion, have mercy on us and on the whole world** (*Diary*, 476). And at the Hour of Great Mercy, we are invited to recall Jesus' Passion and death.

On the Liturgical Calendar, meditating upon the Passion is particularly appropriate on Fridays (as we remember Good Friday), during Lent, and especially during the Sacred Easter Triduum. The devotional prayer par excellence for meditating upon the Lord's Passion is the Stations of the Cross.

It's no surprise then that meditating upon the Passion was so central to the spirituality of St. Faustina, as the Lord Jesus helped her understand more deeply His great mercy for us sinners. He told her, **I desire that you know more profoundly the love that burns in My Heart for souls, and you will understand this when you meditate upon My Passion. Call upon My mercy on behalf of sinners; I desire their salvation** (*Diary*, 186).

Further, in an amazing passage, Jesus tells St. Faustina of the great value of meditating on His Passion even for one hour: **There is more merit to one hour of meditation on My sorrowful Passion than there is to a whole year of flagellation that draws blood; the**

contemplation of My painful wounds is of great profit to you, and it brings Me great joy (*Diary*, 369).

O how much the Lord Jesus loves us, but do we love Him in return, seeking to bring Him great joy?

May these entries on the Passion inspire you to realize in a deeper way how much our Merciful Savior suffered out of love for you. And may you be inspired to make meditation upon His Passion part of your spiritual life.

My Mercy on Behalf of Sinners

Today Jesus said to me, **I desire that you know more profoundly the love that burns in My Heart for souls, and you will understand this when you meditate upon My Passion. Call upon My mercy on behalf of sinners; I desire their salvation. When you say this prayer, with a contrite heart and with faith on behalf of some sinner, I will give him the grace of conversion. This is the prayer:** (*Diary*, 186).

"O Blood and Water, which gushed forth from the Heart of Jesus as a fount of Mercy for us, I trust in You." (*Diary*, 187).

My Prayer Response:

Lord Jesus, may I fulfill Your desire and come to know more deeply Your burning love for souls in Your Passion by meditating on it. Thank You for the Blood and Water, which gushed forth from Your Heart as a fount of mercy for us.

A Share in My Joy and Glory

The Resurrection. Today, during the [Mass of the] Resurrection, I saw the Lord Jesus in the midst of a great light. He approached me and said, **Peace be to you, My children,** and He lifted up His hand and gave His blessing. The wounds in His hands, feet, and side were indelible and shining. When He looked at me with such kindness and love, my whole soul drowned itself in Him. And He said to me, **You have taken a great part in My Passion; therefore I now give you a great share in My joy and glory.** The whole time of the Resurrection [Mass] seemed like only a minute to me. A wondrous recollection filled my soul and lasted throughout the whole festal season. The kindness of Jesus is so great that I cannot express it (*Diary*, 205).

My Prayer Response:

Lord Jesus, I gaze upon You as the Risen Lord through the eyes of St. Faustina — and I contemplate the victory of Your Passion, death, and Resurrection over sin, death, and Satan. May I live in that victory!

More Merit to One Hour

I received permission for one hour of meditation on the Passion of the Lord Jesus and for a certain humiliation. But I was a little dissatisfied at not receiving permission for everything I had asked. When we returned home, I dropped into the chapel for a moment, and then I heard this voice in my soul: **There is more merit to one hour of meditation on My sorrowful Passion than there is to a whole year of flagellation that draws blood; the contemplation of My painful wounds is of great profit to you, and it brings Me great joy** (*Diary*, 369).

[Then Jesus went on to admonish St. Faustina very kindly:]

I am surprised that you still have not completely renounced your self-will, but I rejoice exceedingly that this change will be accomplished during the retreat (*Diary*, 369; see also *Diary*, 371-73).

My Prayer Response:

Lord Jesus, may I grow in humility and surrender to Your divine will by meditating on Your Passion. Your will be done and not mine!

Even Greater Pain

When I came for adoration, an inner recollection took hold of me immediately, and I saw the Lord Jesus tied to a pillar, stripped of His clothes, and the scourging began immediately. I saw four men who took turns at striking the Lord with scourges. My heart almost stopped at the sight of these tortures. The Lord said to me, **I suffer even greater pain than that which you see.** And Jesus gave me to know for what sins He subjected Himself to the scourging: these are sins of impurity. Oh, how dreadful was Jesus' moral suffering during the scourging! (*Diary*, 445).

My Prayer Response:

St. Faustina, through your words, we "see" the Lord Jesus stripped and scourged so cruelly! I'm amazed that Jesus said He suffered even greater pain than what you saw because of our sins of impurity. Lord Jesus, have mercy on us sinners for the pain we have caused You.

See the Human Race

Then Jesus said to me, **Look and see the human race in its present condition.** In an instant, I saw horrible things: the executioners left Jesus, and other people started scourging Him; they seized the scourges and struck the Lord mercilessly. These were priests, religious men and women, and high dignitaries of the Church, which surprised me greatly. There were lay people of all ages and walks of life. All vented their malice on the innocent Jesus. Seeing this, my heart fell as if into a mortal agony. And while the executioners had been scourging Him, Jesus had been silent and looking into the distance; but when those other souls I mentioned scourged Him, Jesus closed His eyes, and a soft but most painful moan escaped from His Heart. And Jesus gave me to know in detail the gravity of the malice of these ungrateful souls: **You see, this is a torture greater than My death.** Then my lips too fell silent, and I began to experience the agony of death … (*Diary*, 445).

My Prayer Response:

Lord Jesus, see the human race in our present condition! We have continued to scourge You. May the pain in my heart over Your pain bring solace to Your Heart.

Sharing in My Pain

Then I saw the Lord Jesus nailed to the cross. When He had hung on it for a while, I saw a multitude of souls crucified like Him. Then I saw a second multitude of souls, and a third. The second multitude were not nailed to [their] crosses, but were holding them firmly in their hands. The third were neither nailed to [their] crosses nor holding them firmly in their hands, but were dragging [their] crosses behind them and were discontent. Jesus then said to me, **Do you see these souls? Those who are like Me in the pain and contempt they suffer will be like Me also in glory. And those who resemble Me less in pain and contempt will also bear less resemblance to Me in glory.**

Among the crucified souls, the most numerous were those of the clergy. I also saw some crucified souls whom I knew, and this gave me great joy (*Diary*, 446).

My Prayer Response:

Lord Jesus, may I daily embrace the cross You give me with joy and thanksgiving for the sake of souls. Help me to unite my pain and miseries with Your Passion.

Seek Light and Strength

When the confessor started talking to me, I did not understand a single word. Then I saw Jesus Crucified and He said to me, **It is in My Passion that you must seek light and strength** (*Diary*, 654).

My Prayer Response with St. Faustina:

After the confession, I meditated on Jesus' terrible Passion, and I understood that what I was suffering was nothing compared to the Savior's Passion, and that even the smallest imperfection was the cause of this terrible suffering. Then my soul was filled with very great contrition, and only then I sensed that I was in the sea of the unfathomable mercy of God. Oh, how few words I have to express what I am experiencing! I feel I am like a drop of dew engulfed in the depths of the bottomless ocean of divine mercy (*Diary*, 654).

With True Feeling

Although I was ill, I made up my mind to make a Holy Hour today as usual. During that hour, I saw the Lord Jesus being scourged at the pillar. In the midst of this frightful torture, Jesus was praying. After a while, He said to me, **There are few souls who contemplate My Passion with true feeling; I give great graces to souls who meditate devoutly on My Passion** (*Diary*, 737).

My Prayer Response:

Lord Jesus, may I meditate devoutly on Your Passion. May I contemplate Your Passion with true feeling. May the graces that I receive by meditating on Your Passion be dispensed to hardened sinners who are most in need of Your mercy.

Infinite Value for Souls

Today, during Mass, I saw the Lord Jesus in the midst of His sufferings, as though dying on the cross. He said to me, **My daughter, meditate frequently on the sufferings which I have undergone for your sake, and then nothing of what you suffer for Me will seem great to you. You please Me most when you meditate on My Sorrowful Passion. Join your little sufferings to My Sorrowful Passion, so that they may have infinite value before My Majesty** (*Diary*, 1512).

My Prayer Response:

Lord Jesus, may I meditate frequently on the sufferings of Your Passion. May I join my little sufferings to Your sorrowful Passion that they may have infinite value for souls.

Disciple of a Crucified Master

Jesus said to me today, **You often call Me your Master. This is pleasing to My Heart; but do not forget, My disciple, that you are a disciple of a crucified Master. Let that one word be enough for you. You know what is contained in the cross** (*Diary*, 1513).

My Prayer Response:

Lord Jesus, my crucified Master, help me to be Your disciple. Help me with Your mercy to offer my daily cross and join it with Your cross and follow You (see Lk 9:23).

A Painful Echo in His Sacred Heart

April 10, 1938. Palm Sunday. I attended Holy Mass, but did not have the strength to go and get the palm. I felt so weak that I barely made it till the end of Mass. During Mass, Jesus gave me to know the pain of His soul, and I could clearly feel how the hymns of *Hosanna* reverberated as a painful echo in His Sacred Heart. My soul, too, was inundated by a sea of bitterness, and each *Hosanna* pierced my own heart to its depths. My whole soul was drawn close to Jesus. I heard Jesus' voice: **My daughter, your compassion for Me refreshes Me. By meditating on My Passion, your soul acquires a distinct beauty** (*Diary*, 1657).

My Prayer Response:

Lord Jesus, may my meditating on Your Passion refresh You and call down Your great mercy on a world that "so needs to understand and accept Divine Mercy" (John Paul II, posthumous Divine Mercy Sunday message, April 3, 2005).

Enter into My Passion

Holy Thursday [April 14, 1938]. Today I felt strong enough to take part in the ceremonies of the Church. During Holy Mass, Jesus stood before me and said, **Look into My Heart and see there the love and mercy which I have for humankind, and especially for sinners. Look, and enter into My Passion.** In an instant, I experienced and lived through the whole Passion of Jesus in my own heart. I was surprised that these tortures did not deprive me of my life (*Diary*, 1663).

My Prayer Response:

Lord Jesus, as I contemplate Your Passion, I see the love and mercy that You have for mankind and especially for sinners. Help me to pause and enter into Your Passion throughout my day.

In All Its Immensity

During adoration, Jesus said to me, **My daughter, know that your ardent love and the compassion you have for Me were a consolation to Me in the Garden** [of Olives] (*Diary*, 1664).

My daughter, today consider My Sorrowful Passion in all its immensity. Consider it as if it had been undertaken for your sake alone (*Diary*, 1761).

My Prayer Response:

Thank You, Lord Jesus, that You would even undergo Your sorrowful Passion for my sake alone:

> I have been crucified with Christ, yet, no longer I, but Christ lives in me; in so far as I now live in the flesh, I live by faith in the Son of God who has loved me and given Himself up for me (Gal 2:19-20).

Eucharist

May 20 – June 8

The Eucharist was central to the life and spirituality of St. Faustina as the source of her union with the Lord, who was the Bridegroom of her soul. She experienced the Real Presence of the Lord Jesus by receiving Him daily in Holy Communion and wrote frequently of the effects of her union with Him in the Eucharist. She goes so far as to say: "My heart is a living tabernacle in which the living Host is reserved. I have never sought God in some far-off place, but within myself. It is in the depths of my own being that I commune with God" (*Diary*, 1302).

As we shall see, Jesus Himself spoke frequently of Holy Communion as the source of St. Faustina's union with Him. He also spoke of His desire to give Himself wholly to her: **Know, My daughter, that the ardor of your heart is pleasing to Me. And just as you desire ardently to become united with Me in Holy Communion, so too do I desire to give Myself wholly to you; and as a reward for your zeal, rest on My Heart** (*Diary*, 826).

Following the custom of Sr. Faustina's religious community, Jesus even providentially arranged for her to pick as her patron "the Most Blessed Sacrament." Thus, she uses "Sister Maria Faustina of the Most Blessed Sacrament" as her full religious name at the beginning of each of the notebooks that make up her *Diary*.

As was the case with St. Faustina, the Eucharist should be at the very heart of our lives as Catholics. But do we prepare well to receive Jesus worthily in Holy Communion, or do we simply go through the motions?

In these entries, Jesus congratulates St. Faustina on her preparation for receiving Him in Holy Communion. But He speaks strongly about those who come to Holy Communion unprepared and unworthily: **I enter into certain hearts as into a second Passion** (*Diary*, 1598).

As you read these passages, examine your own heart. How do you prepare to receive Jesus in Holy Communion? Renew the desire of your heart to prepare well, so you can receive Him worthily — giving joy to His merciful Heart, instead of wounding it.

Jesus with Me

[One time when St. Faustina received Holy Communion, a second Host fell into her hand.]

I desired to rest in your hands, not only in your heart. And at that moment I saw the little Jesus. But when the priest approached, I saw once again only the Host (*Diary*, 160).

One morning after Holy Communion, I heard this voice, **I desire that you accompany Me when I go to the sick** (*Diary*, 183).

My Prayer Response:

Thank You, Jesus, for Your desire to come into my heart in Holy Communion. Increase my desire for You that I may receive You with more fervor. I also pray that the sick would be strengthened by receiving You in Holy Communion.

Unite Yourself with Me

My daughter, do not omit Holy Communion unless you know well that your fall was serious; apart from this, no doubt must stop you from uniting yourself with Me in the mystery of My love. Your minor faults will disappear in My love like a piece of straw thrown into a great furnace. Know that you grieve Me much when you fail to receive Me in Holy Communion (*Diary*, 156).

My Prayer Response:

Lord Jesus, may my minor faults disappear in the fire of Your love when I receive You in Holy Communion. In no way, do I want to grieve You.

The Same Love

Approach each of the sisters with the same love with which you approach Me; and whatever you do for them, you do it for Me (*Diary*, 285).

I am your patron. Read. I looked at once at the inscription and read, "Patron for the Year 1935 — the Most Blessed Eucharist" (*Diary*, 360).

My Prayer Response:

Lord Jesus, help me with Your grace to approach each of my brothers and sisters with the same love I approach You in the Holy Eucharist. What a marvel of grace that would be.

I Am Always with You

I am always in your heart; not only when you receive Me in Holy Communion, but always (*Diary*, 575).

Know, My daughter, that you caused Me more sorrow by not uniting yourself with Me in Holy Communion than you did by that small transgression (*Diary*, 612).

My Prayer Response:

Lord Jesus, thank You for Your constant presence in my heart, even when my heart is veiled with darkness. May I not grieve You by doubting that You are with me always.

My Power

In the Host is your power; It will defend you (*Diary*, 616).

From the ciborium came a voice: **These hosts have been received by souls converted through your prayer and suffering** (*Diary*, 709).

My Prayer Response:

Lord Jesus, may the Eucharist be my power in the battle of life and the power of my intercession for souls. As I receive You in Holy Communion, help me to offer my little sufferings to You for the sake of souls.

The Ardor of Your Heart

Know, My daughter, that the ardor of your heart is pleasing to Me. And just as you desire ardently to become united with Me in Holy Communion, so too do I desire to give Myself wholly to you; and as a reward for your zeal, rest on My Heart (*Diary,* 826).

My Prayer Response:

Lord Jesus, set my heart on fire to receive You with greater desire and fervor. May Your Eucharistic presence be my reward. Let me rest on Your Heart.

Indifferent and Lukewarm Souls

My daughter, write that it pains Me very much when religious souls receive the Sacrament of Love merely out of habit, as if they did not distinguish this food. I find neither faith nor love in their hearts. I go to such souls with great reluctance. It would be better if they did not receive Me (*Diary,* 1288).

My Prayer Response:

Lord Jesus, may my love, faith, and fervor in receiving You in the Eucharist be an ardent prayer for indifferent and lukewarm souls — that You may not be pained. May their hearts be set aflame with love for You.

As a Dead Object

I desire to unite Myself with human souls; My great delight is to unite Myself with souls. Know, My daughter, that when I come to a human heart in Holy Communion, My hands are full of all kinds of graces which I want to give to the soul. But souls do not even pay any attention to Me; they leave Me to Myself and busy themselves with other things. Oh, how sad I am that souls do not recognize Love! They treat Me as a dead object (*Diary*, 1385).

My Prayer Response:

Lord Jesus, I desire to unite myself with You in every Holy Communion and receive all Your graces with fervor. I want to be attentive to You. May my fervor compensate for those who treat You as a dead object!

Stir up a Living Faith

I am the same under each of the species, but not every soul receives Me with the same living faith as you do, My daughter, and therefore I cannot act in their souls as I do in yours (*Diary*, 1407).

My Prayer Response:

Lord Jesus, stir up a living faith in me, so You are free to act in my soul as You desire. I want You to be free to act in my soul as You did in St. Faustina's.

Present in Its Fullness

What you see in reality, these souls see through faith. Oh, how pleasing to Me is their great faith! You see, although there appears to be no trace of life in Me, in reality it is present in its fullness in each and every Host. But for Me to be able to act upon a soul, the soul must have faith. O how pleasing to Me is living faith! (*Diary*, 1420).

My Prayer Response:

Jesus, I do believe, but increase my faith that I may please You even more in each reception of Holy Communion. May I see with the eyes of faith that You are truly present in the Holy Eucharist.

I Wait for Souls

Oh, how painful it is to Me that souls so seldom unite themselves to Me in Holy Communion. I wait for souls, and they are indifferent toward Me. I love them tenderly and sincerely, and they distrust Me. I want to lavish My graces on them, and they do not want to accept them. They treat Me as a dead object, whereas My Heart is full of love and mercy (*Diary*, 1447).

My Prayer Response:

Lord Jesus, help me and all who receive You in Holy Communion to grow in greater trust and love, so we may receive You more tenderly. Lavish Your graces out upon us. May our communion with You truly be a "common — union — in — Christ" and give You great joy.

The Most Tender of Mothers

In order that you may know at least some of My pain, imagine the most tender of mothers who has great love for her children, while those children spurn her love. Consider her pain. No one is in a position to console her. This is but a feeble image and likeness of My love (*Diary,* 1447)**.**

My Prayer Response:

Lord Jesus, I pray that my fervent and loving reception of You in Holy Communion may be a consolation to You. I cannot begin to imagine Your pain when souls receive You indifferently. Help me to love You more deeply and tenderly.

I Get Ingratitude

If the priest had not brought Me to you, I would have come Myself under the same species. My daughter, your sufferings of this night obtained the grace of mercy for an immense number of souls (*Diary,* 1459).

In return for My blessings, I get ingratitude. In return for My love, I get forgetfulness and indifference. My Heart cannot bear this (*Diary,* 1537).

My Prayer Response:

Lord Jesus, through the intercession of St. Faustina, may her great love for You in the Eucharist and her sufferings for souls be a reparation for me and all souls for our lack of gratitude, forgetfulness, and indifference to Your Love in the Holy Eucharist. Saint Faustina, pray for us that we may worthily receive Holy Communion.

A Second Passion

I enter into certain hearts as into a second Passion (*Diary*, 1598).

I enter that heart unwillingly. You received those two Hosts, because I delayed My coming into this soul who resists My grace. My visit to such a soul is not pleasant for Me (*Diary*, 1658).

My Prayer Response:

Lord Jesus, help me to receive Holy Communion with greater love, trust, and desire to live in union with You. I desire to make reparation for certain souls that You describe entering as into a second Passion!

The Hearts of Religious Souls

Write for the benefit of religious souls that it delights Me to come to their hearts in Holy Communion. But if there is anyone else in such a heart, I cannot bear it and quickly leave that heart, taking with Me all the gifts and graces I have prepared for the soul. And the soul does not even notice My going (*Diary*, 1683).

My Prayer Response:

Lord Jesus, make my heart pure and simple as I receive You in Holy Communion. Purify my heart that I may be united more closely with You. And I pray for purity of heart in the souls of religious.

Cleanse Our Hearts

After some time, inner emptiness and dissatisfaction will come to [the soul's] **attention. Oh, if only she would turn to Me then, I would help her to cleanse her heart, and I would fulfill everything in her soul; but without her knowledge and consent, I cannot be the Master of her heart** (*Diary,* 1683).

My Prayer Response:

Lord Jesus, help us turn to You that You may cleanse our hearts. Lord Jesus, meek and humble of Heart, make our hearts like Yours. May we seek to be one heart with You in Holy Communion.

Your Bridegroom

Now you shall consider My love in the Blessed Sacrament. Here, I am entirely yours, soul, body, and divinity, as your Bridegroom. You know what love demands: one thing only, reciprocity ... (*Diary*, 1770).

My daughter, My favor rests in your heart. When on Holy Thursday I left Myself in the Blessed Sacrament, you were very much on My mind (*Diary*, 1774).

My Prayer Response:

Lord Jesus, thank You for total and humble love in giving Yourself to me in the Eucharist. Help me and those who receive You in Holy Communion to respond with "reciprocity." May our "yes" to You be *total, free, faithful, and fruitful* — like the vows of marriage!

A Foretaste of Heaven

See, I have left My heavenly throne to become united with you. What you see is just a tiny part and already your soul swoons with love. How amazed will your heart be when you see Me in all My glory (*Diary,* 1810).

My Prayer Response:

Lord Jesus, Holy Communion here on earth is a foretaste of the heavenly banquet! Help us, O Lord, to fittingly prepare for the eternal banquet by receiving You faithfully and lovingly at each Holy Communion.

Heaven on Earth

... I want to tell you that eternal life must begin already here on earth through Holy Communion. Each Holy Communion makes you more capable of communing with God throughout eternity (*Diary*, 1811).

When I received Him into my heart, the veil of faith was torn away. I saw Jesus who said to me, **My daughter, your love compensates Me for the coldness of many souls.** After these words, I was once again alone, but throughout the whole day I lived in an act of reparation (*Diary*, 1816).

My Prayer Response:

O Lord Jesus, every Holy Communion with You here on earth is already a sharing in the Heavenly Liturgy at the throne of the Father. Help me and all who receive Holy Communion to be ever more capable of communing with You throughout eternity!

Preparation for Communion

During Holy Mass, I saw the Infant Jesus in the chalice, and He said to me. **I am dwelling in your heart as you see Me in this chalice** (*Diary,* 1820).

Most pleasing to Me is this preparation with which you have received Me into your heart. Today, in a special way I bless this your joy. Nothing will disturb that joy throughout this day ... (*Diary,* 1824).

My Prayer Response:

Lord Jesus, help me and all who receive You in Holy Communion with a more fervent preparation, so our hearts may be changed. May we sing this song in our hearts:

> Change my heart, O God,
> Make it ever true.
> Change my heart, O God.
> May I be like You!
> You are the Potter, I am the clay.
> Mold me and make me.
> This is what I pray.

The United Heart of Jesus and St. Faustina

June 9 – 29

In order to understand the united Heart of Jesus and St. Faustina, some background is necessary. In Sacred Scripture and spiritual writings, the "heart" refers to the very center of the person. At times, it is called the higher part of the soul or the *human spirit*.

It is helpful here to understand a key Scripture text of St. Paul: "May the God of peace Himself make you perfectly holy. May you entirely, *spirit, soul, and body*, be preserved blameless for the coming of our Lord Jesus Christ" (1 Thes 5:23, RNAB, *emphasis mine*). Saint Paul is not saying that the "spirit, soul, and body" are three parts of the same person, rather he is saying that each describes the *whole person* in a unique way:

- The body is the whole person as created.
- The soul is the whole person as living and unique.
- The spirit is the whole person in communion with God.

Further, if we think about the spirit, the *heart* is the biblical way of speaking about the human spirit in intimate communion with God. So, when St. Faustina refers to her heart united with the Heart of Jesus, she is describing an intimate union with Jesus.

The Introduction to the "Mass of the Immaculate Heart of Mary" in *Masses of the Blessed Virgin Mary* gives a marvelous description of the meaning of "heart" in this sense of the word:

> The meaning of *"the heart of the Virgin"* is to be understood in a biblical sense: it denotes the person of the Blessed Virgin herself; her intimate and unique being; the *center and source of her interior life*, of her mind and memory, of her will and love; the single-mindedness with which she loved God and the disciples and devoted herself wholeheartedly to the saving work of her Son (*emphasis mine*).

Like the Blessed Virgin Mary, then, St. Faustina sought to be single-minded in loving God and to devote herself wholeheartedly to God. In other words, she sought to unite her heart with that of Jesus as she responded to His love. For instance, in one entry she writes, "I felt the Lord looking into the depths of my heart" (*Diary*, 346).

May we, too, be inspired to unite our heart with the Lord Jesus' Merciful Heart!

Some Notes to the Reader: The first part of these entries begins with a focus on the Heart of Jesus, at times referred to as the Merciful Heart. The second part focuses on the heart of St. Faustina. Further, in a number of entries, the words of St. Faustina before and after Jesus' words are provided to set the context. Finally, some of the entries are divided up over several days because of their length and richness of content.

Console My Heart

On one occasion, Jesus gave me to know that when I pray for intentions which people are wont to entrust to me, He is always ready to grant His graces, but souls do not always want to accept them: **My Heart overflows with great mercy for souls, and especially for poor sinners. If only they could understand that I am the best of Fathers to them and that it is for them that the Blood and Water flowed from My Heart as from a fount overflowing with mercy. For them I dwell in the tabernacle as King of Mercy. I desire to bestow My graces upon souls, but they do not want to accept them. You, at least, come to Me as often as possible and take these graces they do not want to accept. In this way you will console My Heart** (*Diary*, 367).

My Prayer Response:

Lord Jesus, I pray that people who ask for my prayers accept the graces that You mercifully prepare for them in answer to my prayers. May this console Your Heart. Don't let Your graces be wasted — send them to whomever will accept them!

Break through to Souls

Oh, how indifferent are souls to so much goodness, to so many proofs of love! My Heart drinks only of the ingratitude and forgetfulness of souls living in the world. They have time for everything, but they have no time to come to Me for graces (*Diary*, 367).

My Prayer Response:

Lord Jesus, may Your mercy be accepted. May You break through to souls who have no time for You! Soften their stony hearts, O Lord.

So Many Reservations

So I turn to you, you — chosen souls, will you also fail to understand the love of My Heart? Here, too, My Heart finds disappointment; I do not find complete surrender to My love. So many reservations, so much distrust, so much caution (*Diary,* 367).

My Prayer Response:

O Lord Jesus, may I understand and experience the love of Your Heart. May I not disappoint You but completely surrender to Your love with great trust.

Souls Who Love Me Dearly

To comfort you, let Me tell you that there are souls living in the world who love Me dearly. I dwell in their hearts with delight. But they are few. In convents too, there are souls that fill My Heart with joy. They bear My features; therefore the Heavenly Father looks upon them with special pleasure (*Diary*, 367)**.**

My Prayer Response:

Lord Jesus, thank You for telling me that there are souls who live in the world and love You. In Your great mercy, raise up many more souls to love You and give joy to Your Heart. May I be one of them!

A Marvel to Angels and Man

[Souls who love Me dearly] **will be a marvel to Angels and men. Their number is very small. They are a defense for the world before the justice of the Heavenly Father and a means of obtaining mercy for the world. The love and sacrifice of these souls sustain the world in existence. The infidelity of a soul specially chosen by Me wounds My Heart most painfully. Such infidelities are swords which pierce My Heart** (*Diary*, 367).

My Prayer Response:

Lord Jesus, raise up yet more souls who are faithful to Your loving mercy. The world desperately needs their defense of love, their prayers, and their sacrifices. It is a marvel of Your mercy that they sustain the world in existence.

Through the Heart of Jesus

On Friday, during Mass, when my soul was flooded with God's happiness, **I heard these words in my soul: My mercy has passed into souls through the divine-human Heart of Jesus as a ray from the sun passes through crystal.** I felt in my heart and understood that every approach to God is brought about by Jesus, in Him and through Him (*Diary*, 528).

✞ **In this retreat, I shall keep you continually close to My Heart, that you may better know My mercy, that mercy which I have for people and especially for poor sinners** (*Diary*, 730).

My Prayer Response:

Jesus, may the rays of mercy that come from Your Heart shine upon the world and especially on poor sinners. Jesus, have mercy on us and on the whole world.

Close to My Heart

Be at peace, My child. See, you are not alone. My Heart watches over you. Jesus filled me with strength concerning a certain person. I feel strength within my soul (*Diary*, 799).

January 29, 1937. I overslept today. A little longer, and I would have been too late for Holy Communion because the chapel is a good distance from our section. When I went outdoors, the snow was knee-deep. But before it occurred to me that the doctor would not have allowed me to go out in such snow, I had already come to the Lord in the chapel. I received Holy Communion and was back in no time. I heard these words in my soul: **My daughter, rest close to My Heart. Known to Me are your efforts.** My soul is more joyful when I am close to the Heart of my God (*Diary*, 902).

My Prayer Response:

Jesus, thank You for Your Heart that watches over us and knows all our efforts. May I rest close to Your Heart.

My Agonizing Heart

"Jesus, I beg You, by the inconceivable power of Your mercy, that all the souls who will die today escape the fire of hell, even if they have been the greatest sinners. Today is Friday, the memorial of Your bitter agony on the Cross; because Your mercy is inconceivable, the Angels will not be surprised at this." Jesus pressed me to His Heart and said, **My beloved daughter, you have come to know well the depths of My mercy. I will do what you ask, but unite yourself continually with My agonizing Heart and make reparation to My justice. Know that you have asked Me for a great thing, but I see that this was dictated by your pure love for Me; that is why I am complying with your requests** (*Diary,* 873).

My Prayer Response:

Lord Jesus, may I pray with boldness and trust in You as St. Faustina did. May I hear the beautiful words that she heard from You as I make reparation to Your justice!

Rest on My Heart

In the evening, the Lord said to me, **My child, rest on My Heart; I see that you have worked hard in My vineyard.** And my soul was flooded with divine joy (*Diary,* 945).

Today, the Lord visited me, pressed me to His Heart and said, **Rest, My little child. I am always with you** (*Diary,* 1011).

My Prayer Response:

Saint Faustina, intercede for us and teach us how to rest on the Heart of Jesus. We, too, need to be flooded with joy and hear the promise of Jesus, **I am always with you!** (see Mt 28:20).

Delight My Heart

Then I heard a voice in my soul: **Do not cry; I am not suffering any more. And for the faithfulness with which you accompanied Me in My sufferings and death, your own death will be a solemn one, and I will accompany you in that last hour. Beloved pearl of My Heart, I see your love so pure, purer than that of the angels, and all the more so because you keep fighting. For your sake I bless the world. I see your efforts to please Me, and they delight My Heart.**

After these words, I wept no more, but thanked the heavenly Father for having sent us His Son and for the work of the Redemption of mankind (*Diary*, 1061).

My Prayer Response:

Thank You, Heavenly Father, for sending us Your Son for the Redemption of mankind. Thank You, Lord Jesus, for raising up St. Faustina, a pearl of Your Heart, to tell us the good news of Your mercy. Now, may we tell the world of Your mercy and delight Your Heart!

Forgive from the Heart

June 20, [1937]. We resemble God most when we forgive our neighbors. God is Love, Goodness, and Mercy. …

Every soul, and especially the soul of every religious, should reflect My mercy. My Heart overflows with compassion and mercy for all. The heart of My beloved must resemble Mine; from her heart must spring the fountain of My mercy for souls; otherwise I will not acknowledge her as Mine (*Diary,* 1148).

My Prayer Response:

Lord Jesus, may I reflect Your mercy and resemble Your Heart that overflows with compassion and mercy. May I forgive every offense commited against me.

The Wound in My Heart

From all My wounds, like from streams, mercy flows for souls, but the wound in My Heart is the fountain of unfathomable mercy. From this fountain spring all graces for souls. The flames of compassion burn Me. I desire greatly to pour them out upon souls. Speak to the whole world about My mercy (*Diary,* 1190).

My Prayer Response:

Lord, I turn to the wound in Your Heart for all the graces that people need in their miseries. Pour out Your mercy on the whole world. And give me the courage and strength to speak to others about Your mercy.

A Deep Peace

First day. Jesus: **My daughter, this retreat will be an uninterrupted contemplation. I will bring you into this retreat as into a spiritual banquet. Close to My merciful Heart, you will meditate upon all the graces your heart has received, and a deep peace will accompany your soul** (*Diary*, 1327).

My Prayer Response:

Lord, I come close to Your Merciful Heart that I may be nourished as at a spiritual banquet. I so hunger and thirst for Your presence and peace!

Fixed on My Holy Will

I want the eyes of your soul to be always fixed on My holy will, since it is in this way that you will please Me most. No sacrifices can be compared to this. Throughout all the exercises you will remain close to My Heart. You shall not undertake any reforms, because I will dispose of your whole life as I see fit. The priest who will preach the retreat will not speak a single word which will trouble you (*Diary,* 1327).

My Prayer Response:

Lord Jesus, with my spiritual eyes, I want to be always fixed on Your holy will. And help me to remain close to Your Heart. May Your will, not mine, be done.

Every Beat of Your Heart

During Adoration, I heard a voice in my soul: **These efforts of yours, My daughter, are pleasing to Me; they are the delight of My Heart. I see every movement of your heart with which you worship Me** (*Diary,* 1176).

Even among the sisters you will feel lonely. Know then that I want you to unite yourself more closely to Me. I am concerned about every beat of your heart. Every stirring of your love is reflected in My Heart. I thirst for your love (*Diary,* 1542).

My Prayer Response with St. Faustina:

"Yes, O Jesus, but my heart would not be able to live without You, either; for even if the hearts of all creatures were offered to me, they would not satisfy the depths of my heart" (*Diary,* 1542).

Heart of My Heart

When the procession began, I saw Jesus in a brightness greater than the light of the sun. Jesus looked at me with love and said, **Heart of My Heart, be filled with joy.** At that moment my spirit was drowned in Him. … When I came to myself, I was walking along in the procession with the sisters, while my soul was totally immersed in Him … (*Diary,* 1669).

Today, the Lord said to me, **My daughter, look into My Merciful Heart and reflect its compassion in your own heart and in your deeds, so that you, who proclaim My mercy to the world, may yourself be aflame with it** (*Diary,* 1688).

My Prayer Response:

Lord Jesus, as I gaze into Your Merciful Heart, may I reflect Your mercy in my heart and radiate it out to others. May my life be aflame with Your mercy.

Your Heart Is My Repose

At that moment, Jesus suddenly stood before me, coming I know not from where, radiant with unbelievable beauty, clothed in a white garment, with uplifted arms, and He spoke these words to me, **My daughter, your heart is My repose; it is My delight. I find in it everything that is refused Me by so many souls** (*Diary,* 339)**.**

December 24, 1934. The Vigil of Christmas. During the morning Mass, I felt the closeness of God. Though I was hardly aware of it, my spirit was drowned in God. Suddenly, I heard these words: **You are My delightful dwelling place; My Spirit rests in you.** After these words, I felt the Lord looking into the depths of my heart; and seeing my misery, I humbled myself in spirit and admired the immense mercy of God, that the Most High Lord would approach such misery (*Diary,* 346).

My Prayer Response:

Lord Jesus, through the intercession of St. Faustina, may my heart be a place of repose and delight to You! May You find in my heart everything You desire.

You Are in My Heart

During Vespers, I heard these words: **My daughter, I want to repose in your heart, because many souls have thrown Me out of their hearts today. I have experienced sorrow unto death.** I tried to comfort the Lord, by offering Him my love a thousand times over. I felt, within my soul, a great disgust for sin (*Diary*, 866).

During prayer, I heard these words: **My daughter, let your heart be filled with joy. I, the Lord, am with you. Fear nothing. You are in My heart.** At that moment, I knew the great majesty of God, and I understood that nothing could be compared with one single perception of God. Outward greatness dwindles like a speck of dust before one act of a deeper knowledge of God (*Diary*, 1133).

My Prayer Response:

Lord Jesus, I welcome You into my heart. May my heart be a consolation to You today as You fill me with Your joy.

In the Depths of Your Heart

I will tell you most when you converse with Me in the depths of your heart. Here, no one can disturb My actions. Here, I rest as in a garden enclosed (*Diary*, 581).

When you reflect upon what I tell you in the depths of your heart, you profit more than if you had read many books. Oh, if souls would only want to listen to My voice when I am speaking in the depths of their hearts, they would reach the peak of holiness in a short time (*Diary*, 584).

My Prayer Response:

Lord Jesus, teach me. Help me to listen to You as You speak to me in the depths of my heart. Like St. Faustina, help me to become holy as You form my heart to become like Yours.

In Your Arms

On one occasion, I heard these words within me: **Every movement of your heart is known to Me. Know, My daughter, that one glance of yours directed at someone else would wound Me more than many sins committed by another person** (*Diary*, 588).

After Holy Communion, I heard these words in my soul: **I am in your heart, I whom you had in your arms** (*Diary*, 609).

My Prayer Response:

Lord, You know me and You probe me. You know my every thought and desire (see Ps 139). I desire to be the beloved of Your Heart. Bring my every thought and desire "captive in obedience" (2 Cor 10:5) to You. May I be all Yours.

Your Resting Place

I heard a voice coming from the Host: **Here is My repose.** During Benediction, Jesus gave me to know that soon a solemn moment would take place on this very spot. **I am pleased to rest in your heart and nothing will stop Me from granting you graces.** This greatness of God floods my soul, and I drown in Him, I lose myself in Him, I am melting away in Him ... (*Diary*, 1136).

June 1, 1937. Today, the Corpus Christi procession took place. At the first altar, a flame issued from the Host and pierced my heart, and I heard a voice, **Here is My resting place** (*Diary*, 1140).

During Holy Mass, which was celebrated by Father Andrasz, I saw the Infant Jesus who, with hands outstretched toward us, was sitting in the chalice being used at Holy Mass. After gazing at me penetratingly, He spoke these words: **As you see Me in this chalice, so I dwell in your heart** (*Diary*, 1346).

My Prayer Response:

Lord Jesus, dwell in my heart as Your resting place. May nothing in me stop You from granting me graces.

Prayers and Novenas of St. Faustina

June 30 – July 4

We all have our favorite prayers. A number of novenas were prayed by St. Faustina. Two of them were requested by the Lord Jesus: one for her homeland of Poland and the other before the Feast of Mercy.

A novena (Latin for nine) is a set of prayers recited for nine consecutive days. The prayers and intentions vary. The first novena was prayed by the disciples and the Blessed Mother when they gathered in the Upper Room in Jerusalem for nine days to pray for the descent of the Holy Spirit, as promised by Jesus (see Acts 1-2).

For St. Faustina, the novena and prayers for Poland culminated with strong prophetic words of our Lord in regard to Poland. Jesus told her, **I bear a special love for Poland, and if she will be obedient to My will, I will exalt her in might and holiness. From her will come forth the spark that will prepare the world for My final coming** (*Diary*, 1732). What amazing words these are particularly in light of the call of St. Faustina and now the legacy of John Paul II of beloved memory, the Great Mercy Pope.

Further, the Novena before Divine Mercy Sunday has become a major devotion of Divine Mercy apostles (see March 31-April 10 for Jesus' words to St. Faustina about this particular novena). Indeed, Jesus made this astounding promise concerning the novena: **By this novena, I will grant every possible grace to souls** (*Diary*, 796).

We would do well, then, to pray the Novena before Divine Mercy Sunday. Like St. Faustina, we can also be encouraged to remember our own country in prayer, whether it takes the form of a novena or not.

Novena for Poland

1933. On one occasion I heard these words in my soul, **Make a novena for your country. This novena will consist of the recitation of the Litany of the Saints. Ask your confessor for permission** [probably Father Sopocko or Father Andrasz] (*Diary*, 59).

My Prayer Response:

Lord Jesus, our country, too, needs sustained prayer for mercy. Our homeland has become secularized and materialistic. It no longer pays attention to Your moral law, nor does it seek to know You and trust in You. Lord, have mercy on our nation!

Prayer for Our Native Country

♰ Once, after an adoration for our country, a pain pierced my soul, and I began to pray in this way: "Most merciful Jesus, I beseech You through the intercession of Your Saints, and especially the intercession of Your dearest Mother who nurtured You from childhood, bless my native land. I beg You, Jesus, look not on our sins, but on the tears of little children, on the hunger and cold they suffer. Jesus, for the sake of these innocent ones, grant me the grace that I am asking of You for my country." At that moment, I saw the Lord Jesus, His eyes filled with tears, and He said to me, **You see, My daughter, what great compassion I have for them. Know that it is they who uphold the world** (*Diary*, 286).

My Prayer Response:

Lord Jesus, give us a great concern for our native country. Hear our prayer for those who attempt to live without You or those afflicted with poverty and injustice. Especially protect the children — the innocent ones — in our secularized nation.

Joining in Prayer with John Paul II

As I was praying for Poland, I heard the words: **I bear a special love for Poland, and if she will be obedient to My will, I will exalt her in might and holiness. From her will come forth the spark that will prepare the world for My final coming** (*Diary,* 1732).

My Prayer Response with Pope John Paul II:

Pope John Paul II on the occasion of the dedication of the Basilica of The Divine Mercy in Krakow, Poland, August 17, 2002, also entrusted the world to The Divine Mercy. In his reflections, he quoted the above text of the *Diary of St. Faustina* about "the spark" that needs to be lighted by the grace of God — a fire of mercy that needs to be passed on to the world (see *John Paul II: The Great Mercy Pope*, pp. 211-213). In that light, let us join with John Paul II in praying: "May the binding promise of the Lord Jesus be fulfilled. From here there must go forth **the spark that will prepare the world for My final coming.**"

Novena for the Feast of Mercy

Make a novena for the Holy Father's intention. It should consist of thirty-three acts; that is, repetition that many times of the short prayer — which I have taught you — to The Divine Mercy (*Diary,* 341).

"O Blood and Water which gushed forth from the Heart of Jesus as a Fount of Mercy for us, I trust in You" (*Diary,* 309).

[This request of the Lord was in the context of making the Feast of Mercy known (see *Diary,* 341).]

My Prayer Response:

Lord Jesus, now that the Feast of Mercy has been officially declared as a feast day for the whole Church, may it be understood and celebrated throughout the Church. May the Feast of Mercy be an occasion of a flood of mercy poured out on the whole world so desperately in need of Your Divine Mercy!

Novena of Chaplets

The Lord told me to say this chaplet for nine days before the Feast of Mercy. It is to begin on Good Friday. **By this novena, I will grant every possible grace to souls** (*Diary*, 796).

My Prayer Response:

Lord, help us to pray with fervor the Chaplet of The Divine Mercy as we pray the Novena before the Feast of Mercy. Thank You for the gifts of the Novena, the Chaplet of The Divine Mercy, and the Feast of Mercy. What wondrous graces You have promised!

Lukewarm and Indifferent

July 5 – 11

On the final and ninth day of the Novena before the Feast of Mercy, Jesus uses strong words to describe "lukewarm" souls. They can also be called "indifferent." The Lord Jesus says of such souls:

> **Today bring to Me souls who have become lukewarm, and immerse them in the abyss of My mercy. These souls wound My Heart most painfully. My soul suffered the most dreadful loathing in the Garden of Olives because of lukewarm souls, They were the reason I cried out: "Father, take this cup away from Me, if it be Your will." For them, the last hope of salvation is to flee to My mercy** (*Diary*, 1228).

To understand better the lukewarm and indifferent souls Jesus designates for this day, it's interesting that He speaks of His desire elsewhere to completely care for souls and lavish them with great graces. Yet then He notes to St. Faustina, **There are souls who thwart My efforts, but I have not given up on them** (*Diary*, 1682). Then, too, he tells St. Faustina in another place of such lukewarm souls:

> **Souls without love and without devotion, souls full of egoism and self-love, souls full of pride and arrogance, souls full of deceit and hypocrisy, lukewarm souls who have just enough warmth to keep them alive: My Heart cannot bear this. All the graces that I**

pour out upon them flow off them as off the face of a rock, I cannot stand them, because they are neither good nor bad (*Diary,* 1702).

Let us pray for such lukewarm and indifferent souls in the words of St. Faustina from The Divine Mercy Novena prayer. As we do, let's make a commitment to remember them regularly in our prayers:

> Most compassionate Jesus, You are Compassion Itself. I bring lukewarm souls into the abode of Your Most Compassionate Heart. In this fire of Your pure love let these tepid souls, who, like corpses, filled You with such deep loathing, be once again set aflame. O Most Compassionate Jesus, exercise the omnipotence of Your mercy and draw them into the very ardor of Your love, and bestow upon them the gift of holy love, for nothing is beyond Your power.
>
> Eternal Father, turn Your merciful gaze upon lukewarm souls who are nonetheless enfolded in the Most Compassionate Heart of Jesus. Father of Mercy, I beg You by the bitter Passion of Your Son and by His three-hour agony on the Cross: Let them, too, glorify the abyss of Your mercy … (*Diary,* 1229).

Give Us Grateful Hearts

On a certain occasion, the Lord said to me, **I am more deeply wounded by the small imperfections of chosen souls than by the sins of those living in the world.** It made me very sad that chosen souls make Jesus suffer, and Jesus told me, **These little imperfections are not all. I will reveal to you a secret of My Heart: what I suffer from chosen souls. Ingratitude in return for so many graces is My Heart's constant food, on the part of [such] a chosen soul. Their love is lukewarm, and My Heart cannot bear it; these souls force Me to reject them** (*Diary*, 580).

My Prayer Response:

Lord Jesus, forgive the imperfections, the ingratitude, and lukewarm love of souls You have chosen! I beg You have mercy on them and all of us sinners — and bring us to repentance so that we may not continue to make You suffer.

Help Us Trust in Your Goodness

Others distrust My goodness and have no desire to experience that sweet intimacy in their own hearts, but go in search of Me, off in the distance, and do not find Me. This distrust of My goodness hurts Me very much. If My death has not convinced you of My love, what will? Often a soul wounds Me mortally, and then no one can comfort Me. They use My graces to offend Me (*Diary*, 580).

My Prayer Response:

Lord Jesus, have mercy on distrusting souls and forgive them. Give all of us sinners a fresh desire for intimacy with You. Break through with the power of Your cross and love that we may find You in our hearts and not offend You.

Do Not Despise God's Graces

There are souls who despise My graces as well as all the proofs of My love. They do not wish to hear My call, but proceed into the abyss of hell. The loss of these souls plunges Me into deadly sorrow. God though I am, I cannot help such a soul because it scorns Me; having a free will, it can spurn Me or love Me. You, who are the dispenser of My mercy, tell all the world about My goodness, and thus you will comfort My Heart (*Diary*, 580).

My Prayer Response:

Lord Jesus, help all apostles of Divine Mercy to reach souls who despise Your graces and proofs of Your love. Help us to save souls from choosing the abyss of hell — and so comfort Your Heart.

The Spirit of Love

March 1, 1937. The Lord gave me to know how displeased He is with a talkative soul. **I find no rest in such a soul. The constant din tires Me, and in the midst of it the soul cannot discern My voice** (*Diary*, 1008).

Why are You sad today, Jesus? Tell me, who is the cause of Your sadness? And Jesus answered me, **Chosen souls who do not have My spirit, who live according to the letter** [cf. 2 Cor. 3:6] **and have placed the letter above My spirit, above the spirit of love.**

I have founded My whole law on love, and yet I do not see love, even in religious orders. This is why sadness fills My Heart (*Diary*, 1478).

My Prayer Response:

Lord Jesus, help us to discern Your voice within and live according to the spirit of love, so that Your Heart may be filled with joy. We pray for chosen souls who place the letter above Your spirit of love.

Teach Us Silence of Heart

Today, I was talking with the Lord, and He said to me, **There are souls with whom I can do nothing. They are souls that are continuously observing others, but know nothing of what is going on within their own selves. They talk about others continually, even during times of grand silence, which is reserved for speaking only with Me. Poor souls, they do not hear My words; their interior remains empty. They do not look for Me within their own hearts, but in idle talk, where I am never to be found** (*Diary,* 1717).

My Prayer Response:

Lord Jesus, help us to look for You within our hearts. Teach us how to be siilent and listen for Your voice. May we find You, and live in Your presence with awesome awareness and loving attentiveness.

A Call to Humility and Honesty

[These souls with whom I can do nothing] **sense their emptiness, but they do not recognize their own guilt, while souls in whom I reign completely are a constant source of remorse to them. Instead of correcting themselves, their hearts swell with envy, and if they do not come to their senses, they plunge in even deeper. A heart, which thus far is envious, now begins to be filled with hate. And they are already at the edge of the precipice. They are jealous of My gifts in other souls, but they themselves are unable and unwilling to accept them** (*Diary,* 1717).

My Prayer Response:

Lord Jesus, help us to humbly and honestly recognize our own guilt. May we be open to correction from You and others. Help us to turn to You, Lord, with trust and repent when we sin. Help us to reach out to those who have lost their way or are lukewarm and indifferent to Your gifts.

Help Us to Reach Sinners

Tell sinners that no one shall escape My Hand; if they run away from My Merciful Heart, they will fall into My Just Hands. Tell sinners that I am always waiting for them, that I listen intently to the beating of their heart ... when will it beat for Me? Write, that I am speaking to them through their remorse of conscience, through their failures and sufferings, through thunderstorms, through the voice of the Church. And if they bring all My graces to naught, I begin to be angry with them, leaving them alone and giving them what they want (*Diary,* 1728).

My Prayer Response:

Lord Jesus, since no one can escape Your hand, teach us and help us to reach sinners with the good news of Your hand of mercy rather than Your hand of justice. Help us to reach the world desperately in need of Your mercy.

Spiritual Warfare

July 12 – 24

Although she only lived to 33, St. Faustina became a seasoned spiritual warrior in the battle with Satan for souls. After a time of intense spiritual warfare, Jesus told her:

> **You are united to Me; fear nothing. But know, My child, that Satan hates you; he hates every soul, but he burns with a particular hatred for you, because you have snatched many souls from his dominion** (*Diary*, 412).

In her battle for souls, St. Faustina learned that Satan particularly hates God's mercy. She makes two powerful statements about this:

> I have now learned that Satan hates mercy more than anything else, It is his greatest torment (*Diary*, 764).

> How terribly Satan hates God's mercy! I see how he opposes this whole work (*Diary*, 812).

Peter Kreeft, a popular Catholic author on spirituality and apologetics, makes a clear statement about the reality that we are at war, and it is important to know who our enemy is and what our weapons are:

- We are in a spiritual war.
- Our enemy is Satan and his minions.
- Our weapons are the Cross of Christ and the grace and mercy that flows from His

pierced side as Blood and Water.

In this war, Jesus encourages us — as He did St. Faustina — telling us to trust in His mercy **and know that the victory is always on your side** (*Diary,* 1560).

Surrendering to Your Will

Jesus made known to me how very pleasing to Him were prayers of atonement. He said to me, **The prayer of a humble and loving soul disarms the anger of My Father and draws down an ocean of blessings.** After the adoration, half way to my cell, I was surrounded by a pack of huge black dogs who were jumping and howling and trying to tear me to pieces. I realized that they were not dogs, but demons. One of them spoke up in a rage, "Because you have snatched so many souls away from us this night, we will tear you to pieces." I answered, "If that is the will of the most merciful God, tear me to pieces, for I have justly deserved it, because I am the most miserable of all sinners, and God is ever holy, just, and infinitely merciful." To these words all the demons answered as one, "Let us flee, for she is not alone; the Almighty is with her!" (*Diary,* 320).

My Prayer Response:

Thank You, Lord, for teaching me an effective response to spiritual attacks as demonstrated by St. Faustina. She responded by surrendering to Your will. May I always humbly obey Your will.

Suffering and Praying for Souls

[Sister Faustina was vexed by demons during the night, one of them took the form of a cat, jumping onto her bed:]

I kept praying the rosary all the while, and toward dawn these beings vanished, and I was able to get some sleep. When I entered the chapel in the morning I heard a voice in my soul, **You are united to Me; fear nothing. But know, My child, that Satan hates you; he hates every soul, but he burns with a particular hatred for you, because you have snatched so many souls from his dominion** (*Diary,* 412).

My Prayer Response:

Thank You, Lord Jesus, for Your word of warning: Satan hated St. Faustina because she snatched so many souls from his dominion. Please protect us as we suffer and pray for the salvation of souls.

Help Me Withstand Temptations

[St. Faustina was tempted repeatedly by Satan against her vocation of proclaiming God's mercy and praying for mercy for souls, especially sinners (see *Diary*, 1496-1499):]

At that moment, I saw Jesus, who said, **I am pleased with what you are doing. And you can continue to be at peace if you always do the best you can in respect to this work of mercy. Be absolutely as frank as possible with your confessor.**

Satan gained nothing by tempting you, because you did not enter into conversation with him. Continue to act in this way. You gave Me great glory today by fighting so faithfully (*Diary*, 1499).

My Prayer Response:

Lord, may I be faithful to my vocation at times of temptation. May I not enter into temptation by conversation with the Evil One. By the grace of Your presence, help me to withstand temptations.

Directives about Temptations

February 3, [1938]. Today after Holy Communion, Jesus again gave me a few directives: **First, do not fight against a temptation by yourself, but disclose it to the confessor at once, and then the temptation will lose all its force. Second, during these ordeals do not lose your peace; live in My presence; ask My Mother and the Saints for help** (*Diary*, 1560).

My Prayer Response:

Thank You, Lord, for giving me directives about temptations. May I always be open with my confessor. May I remain at peace in the midst of temptation by living in Your presence and asking Mother Mary and the Saints for help.

More Directives

Third, have the certitude that I am looking at you and supporting you. Fourth, do not fear either struggles of the soul or any temptations, because I am supporting you; if only you are willing to fight, know that the victory is always on your side. Fifth, know that by fighting bravely you give Me great glory and amass merits for yourself. Temptation gives you a chance to show Me your fidelity (*Diary*, 1560).

My Prayer Response:

Lord Jesus, thank You, for Your encouragement and support in fighting temptations. May I give You great glory in fighting temptations and show You my fidelity.

The Work of Redemption

Listen, My daughter, although all the works that come into being by My will are exposed to great sufferings, consider whether any of them has been subject to greater difficulties than that work which is directly Mine — the work of Redemption. You should not worry too much about adversities. The world is not as powerful as it seems to be; its strength is strictly limited (*Diary*, 1643).

My Prayer Response:

Lord Jesus, may I not worry and lose my peace when I face difficulties in promoting Your mercy to souls in need. May I be inspired in the struggle by the words of the Great Mercy Pope: "The ultimate limit to evil is Divine Mercy" (see Pope John Paul II, *Memory and Identity*, p. 55).

Like Fog before the Sun's Rays

Know, My daughter, that if your soul is filled with the fire of My pure love, then all difficulties dissipate like fog before the sun's rays and dare not touch the soul. All adversaries are afraid to start a quarrel with such a soul, because they sense that it is stronger than the whole world … (*Diary*, 1643).

My Prayer Response:

Lord Jesus, may I be filled with the "fire of mercy" (Pope John Paul II, Krakow, Poland, August 17, 2002, Entrustment of the World to Divine Mercy) and watch all difficulties to promoting Divine Mercy disappear like fog in the sun's rays. I trust in Your mercy.

Part One of Conference

Conference on Spiritual Warfare.

My daughter, I want to teach you about spiritual warfare. Never trust in yourself, but abandon yourself totally to My will. In desolation, darkness, and various doubts, have recourse to Me and to your spiritual director. He will always answer you in My name. Do not bargain with any temptation; lock yourself immediately in My Heart and, at the first opportunity, reveal the temptation to the confessor (*Diary,* 1760).

My Prayer Response:

Thank You, Jesus, for Your conference on spiritual warfare. May Your teachings sink deeply into my heart and mind. May I place my trust in You and abandon myself to Your will, locking myself in Your Heart. Remind me at the first opportunity to reveal the temptations to my confessor.

Part Two of Conference

Conference on Spiritual Warfare.

Put your self-love in the last place, so that it does not taint your deeds. Bear with yourself with great patience. Do not neglect interior mortifications. Always justify to yourself the opinions of your superiors and of your confessor. Shun murmurers like a plague. Let all act as they like; you are to act as I want you to (*Diary,* 1760).

My Prayer Response:

Thank You, Lord, for teaching me about my personal response in spiritual warfare: to set aside self-love, be patient, and make use of mortifications. May I act as You want me to.

Part Three of Conference

Conference on Spiritual Warfare.

Observe the rule as faithfully as you can. If someone causes you trouble, think what good you can do for the person who caused you to suffer. Do not pour out your feelings. Be silent when you are rebuked. Do not ask everyone's opinion, but only the opinion of your confessor; be as frank and simple as a child with him (*Diary,* 1760).

My Prayer Response:

Lord Jesus, thank You, for encouraging me to be faithful to my vocation in the midst of spiritual warfare. Help me to keep these points in mind: consider what good I can do to the person who caused me to suffer; not to pour out my feelings; and to be silent when rebuked.

Part Four of Conference

Conference on Spiritual Warfare.

Do not become discouraged by ingratitude. Do not examine with curiosity the roads down which I lead you. When boredom and discouragement beat against your heart, run away from yourself and hide in My Heart. Do not fear struggle; courage itself often intimidates temptations, and they dare not attack us (*Diary,* 1760).

My Prayer Response:

Thank You, Lord, for the instruction on what to do when discouragement, fatique, and struggles come upon me. Help me to run away from myself and hide in Your Heart. Give me courage in the midst of the struggle.

Part Five of Conference

Conference on Spiritual Warfare.

Always fight with the deep conviction that I am with you. Do not be guided by feeling, because it is not always under your control; but all merit lies in the will. Always depend upon your superiors, even in the smallest things. I will not delude you with prospects of peace and consolations; on the contrary, prepare for great battles. Know that you are now on a great stage where all heaven and earth are watching you. Fight like a knight, so that I can reward you. Do not be unduly fearful, because you are not alone (*Diary,* 1760).

My Prayer Response:

Thank You, Lord, for Your conference on spiritual warfare. Promoting Your message of Divine Mercy is a great battle, but with Your grace and presence, I want to fight like a knight!

Experienced in Battle

Jesus, Savior, who have deigned to come into my heart, drive away these distractions which are keeping me from talking to You.

Jesus answered me, **I want you to become like a knight experienced in battle, who can give orders to others amid the exploding shells. In the same way, My child, you should know how to master yourself amid the greatest difficulties, and let nothing drive you away from Me, not even your falls** (*Diary,* 1823).

My Prayer Response:

Lord Jesus, Your coming into my heart by Holy Communion strengthens me to enter into the battle of promoting Your message of The Divine Mercy. Help me to become experienced in battle. May I always be faithful to You.

Strive for Sanctity

July 25 – 31

Saint Faustina writes that from her earliest years, she wanted to be a great saint. She wanted to love God as no one had ever loved Him (see *Diary,* 1372). She made clear that she wanted to become a saint in spite of everything, that is, in spite of her wretchedness, "I want to become a saint, and I trust that God's mercy can make a saint even out of such misery as I am, because I am utterly in good will. In spite of all my defeats, I want to go on fighting like a holy soul and to comport myself like a holy soul" (*Diary,* 1333). And she said, "I strive for the greatest perfection possible in order to be useful to the Church" (*Diary,* 1475).

I especially like St. Faustina's description on how easy it is to become a saint. It comes just after she has suffered great pain for a particular soul:

> On a certain occasion, I saw a person about to commit a mortal sin. I asked the Lord to send me the greatest torments so that that soul could be saved. Then I suddenly felt the terrible pain of a crown of thorns on my head. It lasted for quite a long time, but that person remained in the Lord's grace. O my Jesus, how very easy it is to become holy; all that is needed is a bit of good will. If Jesus sees this little bit of good will in the soul, He hurries to give Himself to the soul, and nothing can stop Him, neither shortcomings nor falls — absolutely nothing. Jesus is anxious to help that soul, and if it is faithful to this grace

> from God, it can very soon attain the highest holiness possible for a creature here on earth. God is very generous and does not deny His grace to anyone. Indeed He gives more than what we ask of Him. Faithfulness to the inspirations of the Holy Spirit — that is the shortest route (*Diary*, 291).

I love St. Faustina's final statement in this passage: "The shortest route" to holiness is "faithfulness to the inspirations of the Holy Spirit." Lord, by Your grace, may we always be faithful to the inspirations of the Holy Spirit. Lord, make us saints!

The Lord's Exhortation

Know this, My daughter: if you strive for perfection you will sanctify many souls; and if you do not strive for sanctity, by the same token, many souls will remain imperfect. Know that their perfection will depend on your perfection, and the greater part of the responsibility for these souls will fall on you (*Diary*, 1165).

My Prayer Response:

Thank you, St. Faustina, for listening to and obeying the Lord by striving for great sanctity. May I and all the readers of this exhortation of the Lord follow your example of striving for great sanctity. Lord, give us the grace to be saints like St. Faustina.

This Firm Resolution

This firm resolution to become a saint is extremely pleasing to Me. I bless your efforts and will give you opportunities to sanctify yourself. Be watchful that you lose no opportunity that My providence offers you for sanctification (*Diary*, 1361).

My Prayer Response:

Lord, bless my efforts to become a saint and so please You. May I take advantage of the opportunities You give me to grow in sanctity. Help me to be watchful for every opportunity.

Called to Humility

If you do not succeed in taking advantage of an opportunity, do not lose your peace, but humble yourself profoundly before Me and, with great trust, immerse yourself completely in My mercy. In this way, you gain more than you have lost, because more favor is granted to a humble soul than the soul itself asks for ... (*Diary,* 1361).

My Prayer Response:

Lord Jesus, help me to remain in peace, even when I struggle. May I rejoice in my humiliation and turn to Your mercy with even greater trust. May I give You thanks for Your mercy.

It Is All Grace

I have noticed that, from the very moment I entered the convent, I have been charged with one thing; namely, that I am a saint. But this word was always used scoffingly. At first, this hurt me very much, but when I had risen above it, I paid no attention to it. However, when on one occasion a certain person [perhaps Father Sopocko] suffered because of my sanctity, I was very pained that, because of me, others can experience some unpleasantness. And I began to complain to the Lord Jesus, asking why this should be so, and the Lord answered me, **Are you sad because of this? Of course, you are a saint. Soon I Myself will make this manifest in you, and they will pronounce the same word,** *saint,* only this time it will be with love (*Diary,* 1571).

My Prayer Response:

Lord Jesus, help me not to be ashamed of my striving for sanctity. Sanctity is all Your gift; it is all grace. Remind me that sanctity is not a private love affair with You, Lord — You have called all of us to "be holy, because I am holy" (1 Pet 1:16; Lev 10:2).

The Light of Holiness

Chosen souls are, in My hand, lights which I cast into the darkness of the world and with which I illumine it. As stars illumine the night, so chosen souls illumine the earth. And the more perfect a soul is, the stronger and the more far-reaching is the light shed by it. It can be hidden and unknown, even to those closest to it, and yet its holiness is reflected in souls even to the most distant extremities of the world (*Diary,* 1601).

My Prayer Response:

Lord Jesus, You told us through St. John: "I am the light of the world. No follower of Mine shall ever walk in darkness; no, he shall possess the light of life" (Jn 8:12). And so You also taught us: "You are the light of the world" (Mt 5:14). Thank You for teaching us through St. Faustina that the greater the sanctity of souls, the more the light of holiness is reflected around the world.

You are That Saint

First Friday. When I took the *Messenger of the Sacred Heart* into my hand and read the account of the canonization of Saint Andrew Bobola, my soul was instantly filled with a great longing that our Congregation, too, might have a saint, and I wept like a child that there was no saint in our midst. And I said to the Lord, "I know Your generosity, and yet it seems to me that You are less generous toward us." … And the Lord Jesus said to me, **Don't cry. You are that saint.** Then the light of God inundated my soul, and I was given to know how much I was to suffer, and I said to the Lord, "How will that come about? You have been speaking to me about another Congregation." And the Lord answered, **It is not for you to know how this will come about. Your duty is to be faithful to My grace and to do always what is within your power and what obedience allows you to do …** (*Diary*, 1650).

My Prayer Response:

Thank you, St. Faustina, for evoking the word of the Lord: **You are that saint**. Thank you, St. Faustina, for your holy life and your *Diary*.

Completely in My Care

May 1, [1938]. This evening, Jesus said to me, **My daughter, do you need anything?** I answered, "O my Love, when I have You I have everything." And the Lord answered, **If souls would put themselves completely in My care, I Myself would undertake the task of sanctifying them, and I would lavish even greater graces on them. There are souls who thwart My efforts, but I have not given up on them; as often as they turn to Me, I hurry to their aid, shielding them with My mercy, and I give them the first place in My compassionate Heart** (*Diary,* 1682).

My Prayer Response:

Lord Jesus, I desire to put myself completely in Your care. Please undertake the task of sanctifying me. Without Your grace, I can do nothing! But with Your grace, I can do anything, because then all things are possible: "In Him I have strength for everything through Him who empowers me" (Phil 4:13).

Graces of Retreats

August 1 – 18

As a religious sister, St. Faustina made a number of retreats with her community. She made the annual eight-day retreats, the monthly retreat days, special retreats before final vows, and when asked by the Lord. They were times of prayer and spiritual conferences during which she was blessed with special graces from the Lord.

She recorded the graces of her retreats in the *Diary.* For example, before one of her retreats, the Lord Jesus told her, **My daughter, I am preparing many graces for you, which you will receive during this retreat which will begin tomorrow** (*Diary,* 167).

The Lord would even give specific direction for a particular retreat. On one occasion, she was preparing to go on retreat and was struggling with doubts about the message of Divine Mercy Jesus had given her. Jesus told her before the retreat:

> **And as a proof that it is I who am speaking to you, you will go to confession on the second day of the retreat to the priest who is preaching the retreat; you will go to him as soon as he has finished his conference and will present to him all your doubts concerning Me. I will answer you through his lips, and then your fears will end. During this retreat, observe such strict silence that it will be as though nothing exists around you. You shall speak only to Me and to your**

confessor; you will ask your superiors only for penances (*Diary*, 169).

As we read these entries, we can be encouraged to make retreats as our state of life and circumstances allow. These entries can also encourage us to seek God's direction and His graces in our everyday lives. Each day can be like a retreat with the Lord.

Comfort of My Heart

Probation Before Perpetual Vows

When I learned I was to go for probation [testing], my heart beat with joy at the thought of such an immense grace, that of the perpetual vows. I went before the Blessed Sacrament; and when I immersed myself in a prayer of thanksgiving, I heard these words in my soul: **My child, you are My delight, you are the comfort of My Heart. I grant you as many graces as you can hold. As often as you want to make Me happy, speak to the world about My great and unfathomable mercy** (*Diary,* 164).

My Prayer Response:

Lord Jesus, may we, too, make You happy as we **speak to the world about** [Your] **great and unfathomable mercy**. May we, too, delight You and comfort You by our trust in Your mercy.

This Grace Is Being Given

A few weeks before I was told about the probation, I entered the chapel for a moment and Jesus said to me, **At this very moment the superiors are deciding which sisters are going to take perpetual vows. Not all of them will be granted this grace, but this is their own fault. He who does not take advantage of small graces will not receive great ones. But to you, My child, this grace is being given** (*Diary,* 165).

My Prayer Response:

Lord Jesus, may we, like St. Faustina, take advantage of small graces. Help us to be faithful in receiving Your graces with thanksgiving and sharing them with others.

Jesus Arranges the Circumstances

My daughter, I desire that your heart be formed after the model of My merciful Heart. You must be completely imbued with My mercy (*Diary,* 167).

My daughter, I am preparing many graces for you, which you will receive during this retreat which you will begin tomorrow. I answered, "Jesus, the retreat has already begun, and I am not supposed to go." And He said to me, **Get ready for it, because you will begin the retreat tomorrow. And as for your departure, I will arrange that with the superiors** (*Diary,* 167).

My Prayer Response:

Lord Jesus, I desire to model my heart after Your Merciful Heart — so I ask You to form my heart. As you arranged the retreat for St. Faustina, so arrange the circumstances in my life in order to accomplish Your work within me. Lord Jesus, meek and humble of Heart, make my heart like Yours that I may be infused with Your mercy.

The Gift of Profound Peace

My conversation with the Lord Jesus before the retreat. Jesus told me that this retreat would be a little different from others. **You shall strive to maintain a profound peace in respect to your communings with Me. I will remove all doubts in this regard. I know that you are at peace now as I speak to you, but the moment I stop talking you will start looking for doubts. But I want you to know that I will affirm your soul to such a degree that even if you wanted to be troubled, it will not be within your power** (*Diary,* 169).

My Prayer Response:

Lord Jesus, I love the way You described Your gift of peace to St. Faustina. I would love to receive that kind of peace! So I ask You: Fill me with *Your* peace that I may be at peace.

Bless Our Confessors

And as a proof that it is I who am speaking to you, you will go to confession on the second day of the retreat to the priest who is preaching the retreat; you will go to him as soon as he has finished his conference and will present to him all your doubts concerning Me. I will answer you through his lips, and then your fears will end. During this retreat, observe such strict silence that it will be as though nothing exists around you. You shall speak only to Me and to your confessor; you will ask your superiors only for penances. I felt immense joy that the Lord would show me such kindness and lower Himself so much for my sake (*Diary*, 169).

My Prayer Response:

Lord Jesus, I ask You to bless our confessors. Bless them with Your wisdom and answers to our doubts and concerns. Bless our retreat masters that they may speak Your word in answer to our needs.

You Are Sovereign

During this retreat, I Myself will direct your soul. I want to confirm you in peace and love. And so, the first few days passed by. On the fourth day, doubts began to trouble me: Is not this tranquillity of mine false? Then I heard these words, **My daughter, imagine that you are the sovereign of all the world and have the power to dispose of all things according to your good pleasure. You have the power to do all the good you want, and suddenly a little child knocks on your door, all trembling and in tears and, trusting in your kindness, asks for a piece of bread lest he die of starvation. What would you do for this child? Answer Me, My daughter.** And I said, "Jesus, I would give the child all it asked and a thousand times more" (*Diary*, 229).

My Prayer Response:

Lord Jesus, thank You for directing our souls in times of retreat and prayer. Since You are sovereign over the whole world, direct our prayer and lives according to Your will. Thank You for Your astounding goodness to us in our need.

Confirmed in Love

In this retreat I am giving you, not only peace, but also such a disposition of soul that even if you wanted to experience uneasiness you could not do so. My love has taken possession of your soul, and I want you to be confirmed in it. Bring your ear close to My Heart, forget everything else, and meditate upon My wondrous mercy. My love will give you the strength and courage you need in these matters (*Diary*, 229).

My Prayer Response:

Thank You, Lord Jesus, for Your gift of peace. Take possession of my heart with Your love. Help me to meditate on Your wondrous mercy that gives me strength and courage.

Your Heart Is My Heaven

[In the evening of April 30, 1933, before Perpetual vows.]

My daughter, your heart is My heaven (*Diary*, 238).

The words of Jesus during my perpetual vows: **My spouse, our hearts are joined forever. Remember to whom you have vowed** … everything cannot be put into words (*Diary*, 239).

My Prayer Response:

Lord Jesus, make my heart Your heaven. May my heart be joined with You forever. Saint Faustina, intercede for me that I may be one heart with the Heart of Jesus.

Like Jesus in Suffering and Humility

[October 11, 1933, after a three-hour struggle in adoration, Jesus in His Passion appeared to St. Faustina.]

The bride must resemble her Betrothed. I understood these words to their very depth. There is no room for doubt here. My likeness to Jesus must be through suffering and humility.

See what love of human souls has done to Me. My daughter, in your heart I find everything that so great a number of souls refuses Me. Your heart is My repose. I often wait with great graces until towards the end of prayer (*Diary,* 268).

My Prayer Response:

Lord Jesus, bless those who are in struggles with the gift of perseverance in their prayer. May our hearts be a repose in Your agony over those who refuse You. May we be like You through suffering and humility.

Witnesses of Your Infinite Mercy

During one conference, Jesus said to me, **You are a sweet grape in a chosen cluster; I want others to have a share in the juice that is flowing within you** (*Diary,* 393).

I suddenly saw the Lord Jesus, radiant with unspeakable beauty, and He said to me with kindness, **My chosen one, I will give you even greater graces that you may be the witness of My infinite mercy throughout all eternity** (*Diary,* 400).

My Prayer Response:

Lord Jesus, make us witnesses of Your infinite mercy. Help us to share Your radiant mercy with our brothers and sisters that they, too, may experience Your mercy.

Fearless Apostles of Divine Mercy

On the evening of the introductory day of the retreat, as I listened to the points for the meditation, I heard these words: **During this retreat I will speak to you through the mouth of this priest to strengthen you and assure you of the truth of the words which I address to you in the depths of your soul. Although this is a retreat for all the sisters, I have you especially in mind, as I want to strengthen you and make you fearless in the midst of all the adversities which lie ahead. Therefore, listen intently to his words and meditate upon them in the depths of your soul** (*Diary*, 456).

My Prayer Response:

Lord, strengthen us with the words of preachers and teachers to assure us of the words that You speak in the depth of our hearts. Make us fearless apostles of Divine Mercy who are emboldened to "speak the truth in love" (Eph 4:15).

A Pliant Tool

Once after Holy Communion, I heard these words: **You are Our dwelling place.** At that moment, I felt in my soul the presence of the *Holy Trinity*, the Father, the Son, and the Holy Spirit. I felt that I was the temple of God. I felt I was a child of the Father. I cannot explain all this, but the spirit understands it well. O Infinite Goodness, how low You stoop to Your miserable creature! (*Diary,* 451).

Bear in mind that when you come out of this retreat, I shall be dealing with you as with a perfect soul. I want to hold you in My hand as a pliant tool, perfectly adapted to the completion of My works (*Diary,* 1359).

My Prayer Response:

Lord Jesus, may I feel the presence of the Most Holy Trinity within me as Your temple, and so be Your tool to do Your work of mercy. O Lord, make me a pliant tool in Your hand. All for Your glory!

Responding Faithfully to Your Grace

As I was trying to make my Holy Hour, I saw the suffering Jesus, who spoke these words to me: **My daughter, do not pay so much attention to the vessel of grace as to the grace itself which I give you, because you are not always pleased with the vessel, and then the graces, too, become deficient. I want to guard you from that, and I want you never to pay attention to the vessel in which I send you My grace. Let all the attention of your soul be concentrated on responding to My grace as faithfully as possible** (*Diary*, 1599).

My Prayer Response:

Lord Jesus, may I recognize Your grace, no matter how it comes to me. Guard me from distractions. May I receive Your grace faithfully with thanksgiving, so You may be glorified.

Lavish New Graces on Us

After Holy Mass, I went out to the garden to make my meditation … .

Suddenly Jesus stood before me and said, **What are you doing here so early?** I answered, "I am thinking of You, of Your mercy and Your goodness toward us. And You, Jesus, what are You doing here?" **I have come out to meet you, to lavish new graces on you. I am looking for souls who would like to receive My grace** (*Diary*, 1705).

My Prayer Response:

Lord Jesus, help me to recognize and receive Your graces with joy. I need all the graces that You want to lavish on me!

Send Forth Your Spirit

Today the Lord said to me, **You shall make a three-day retreat before the coming of the Holy Spirit. I Myself will direct you. You shall not follow any of the rules required for retreats or use any books for meditation. Your task is to listen attentively to My words. For spiritual reading you shall read one chapter from the Gospel of St. John** (*Diary*, 1709).

My Prayer Response:

Lord Jesus, bless me with Your Holy Spirit. I want to claim all of the five promises You made of sending the Holy Spirit in the Gospel of St. John (see 14:16-17; 14:26; 15:26; 16:7-11; 16:13-15). Lord, send forth Your Spirit and renew the face of the earth.

Daily Bread for Me

In the evening, Jesus gave me the subject for meditation. At the first moment, my heart was filled with fear and joy. Then I pressed myself close to His Heart, and the fear vanished; only joy remained. I felt entirely like a child of God, and the Lord said to me, **Fear nothing. What has been forbidden to others has been given to you. The graces that are not given to other souls to discern, not even from a distance, nourish you every day, like the daily bread** (*Diary,* 1753).

My Prayer Response:

Lord Jesus, I press close to Your Heart that my fear may vanish. Like a child, I want to receive all the graces You have prepared for me! May Your graces nourish me like daily bread.

The Lamb of God

Consider, My daughter, who it is to whom your heart is so closely united by the vows. Before I made the world, I loved you with the love your heart is experiencing today and, throughout the centuries, My love will never change (*Diary,* 1754).

My Prayer Response:

Lord Jesus, may I experience now the love with which You loved me before You made the world. May I experience especially the love You expressed in Your Passion, death on the cross, and Resurrection. You are the Lamb of God who takes away the sins of the world.

The Gift of the Church

My daughter, consider the life of God which is found in the Church for the salvation and the sanctification of your soul. Consider the use that you make of these treasures of grace, of these efforts of My love (*Diary,* 1758).

My Prayer Response:

Thank You, Lord Jesus, for the treasure of graces You have given the Church for our salvation and sanctification. Thank You for the graces of Your Sacraments, culminating in the Holy Eucharist; for the Communion of Saints with Our Blessed Mother as Queen of all Saints; for the shepherds You have provided for us, with our chief shepherd, the Successor of Peter. All these treasures of grace are a gift of Your merciful love.

Tell My Priests

August 19 – 23

The entries in this section are also included in other sections of *Divine Mercy Minutes with Jesus*. They are intentionally repeated here with a focus on priests, because of the importance of priests in making known to souls Jesus' desire to show them mercy, while it is still time for mercy. Priests are particularly called to preach about God's mercy on Divine Mercy Sunday. As Jesus told St. Faustina:

> **No soul will be justified until it turns with confidence to My mercy, and this is why the first Sunday after Easter is to be the Feast of Mercy. On that day, priests are to tell everyone about My great and unfathomable mercy. I am making you the** [dispenser] **of My mercy** (*Diary*, 570)**.**

Recognizing the importance of priests and their ministry of mercy, St. Faustina faithfully prayed for them. She recorded her prayer for priests, which I love to pray daily:

> O my Jesus, I beg You on behalf of the whole Church: Grant it love and the light of Your Spirit, and give power to the words of priests so that hardened hearts might be brought to repentance and return to You, O Lord. Lord, give us holy priests; You Yourself maintain them in holiness. O Divine and Great High Priest, may the power of Your mercy accompany them everywhere and protect them

> from the devil's traps and snares which are continually being set for the souls of priests. May the power of Your mercy, O Lord, shatter and bring to naught all that might tarnish the sanctity of priests, for You can do all things (*Diary,* 1052).

Along with praying for priests, St. Faustina would offer up her suffering for them:

> December 17 [1936]. I have offered up this day for priests. I have suffered more today than ever before, both interiorly and exteriorly. I did not know it was possible to suffer so much in one day. I tried to make a Holy Hour, in the course of which my spirit had a taste of the bitterness of the Garden of Gethsemane. I am fighting alone, supported by His arm, against all the difficulties that face me like unassailable walls. But I trust in the power of His name and I fear nothing (*Diary,* 823).

We, too, can be encouraged to pray regularly for our priests, especially our pastor and confessor, and to offer our suffering for them.

Priests Are to Proclain Mercy

I desire that priests proclaim this great mercy of Mine towards souls of sinners. Let the sinner not be afraid to approach Me. The flames of mercy are burning Me — clamoring to be spent; I want to pour them out upon these souls (*Diary,* 50)**.**

My Prayer Response:

Lord Jesus, bless priests with Your great gift of mercy, so they may radiate Your mercy in preaching and in the confessional. May Your mercy draw sinners to the feet of Your representatives to receive grace from the fountain of Your mercy.

Speak to Priests of Mercy

My daughter, speak to priests about this inconceivable mercy of Mine. The flames of mercy are burning Me — clamoring to be spent; I want to keep pouring them out upon souls; souls just don't want to believe in My goodness (*Diary,* 177).

My Prayer Response:

Lord Jesus, may the flames of Your mercy set priests on fire with Your inconceivable mercy, so lukewarm and unbelieving souls may be set ablaze with Your mercy through the ministry of priests.

Pray for Priests

No soul will be justified until it turns with confidence to My mercy, and this is why the first Sunday after Easter is to be the Feast of Mercy. On that day, priests are to tell everyone about My great and unfathomable mercy. I am making you the [dispenser] **of My mercy** (*Diary*, 570).

Today, I saw the Lord in great beauty, and He said to me, **My loving host, pray for priests, especially during this time of harvest. My Heart is pleased with you, and for your sake I am blessing the earth** (*Diary*, 980).

My Prayer Response:

Lord Jesus, inspire priests with Your love and mercy, so when they preach — especially on the Feast of Mercy — the people may receive Your great and unfathomable mercy. Remind me, Lord, to pray for priests, especially during this time of harvest.

Recommend the Chaplet to Sinners

I heard these words in my soul: **Say unceasingly the chaplet that I have taught you. Whoever will recite it will receive great mercy at the hour of death. Priests will recommend it to sinners as their last hope of salvation. Even if there were a sinner most hardened, if he were to recite this chaplet only once, he would receive grace from My infinite mercy. I desire that the whole world know My infinite mercy. I desire to grant unimaginable graces to those souls who trust in My mercy** (*Diary*, 687).

My Prayer Response:

Lord Jesus, teach priests to love and pray the Chaplet of Divine Mercy. May they recommend it to sinners as their last hope of salvation and to all at the hour of death so as to receive great mercy.

Hardened Sinners Will Repent

The Lord said to me, **My daughter, do not tire of proclaiming My mercy. In this way you will refresh this Heart of Mine, which burns with a flame of pity for sinners. Tell My priests that hardened sinners will repent on hearing their words when they speak about My unfathomable mercy, about the compassion I have for them in My Heart. To priests who proclaim and extol My mercy, I will give wondrous power; I will anoint their words and touch the hearts of those to whom they will speak** (*Diary*, 1521).

My Prayer Response:

Lord, what a fantastic promise to priests who proclaim and extol Your mercy! Awaken priests to receive Your wondrous power that anoints their words and touches the hearts of their congregation. Please do it, Lord; the Church and world desperately need Your mercy now while it is time for mercy!

Confession

August 24 – September 2

Our current name for confession is the Sacrament of Reconciliation or Penance. Our Lord Jesus used several titles for this Sacrament when speaking to St. Faustina: "Tribunal of My mercy," "Fountain of My mercy," "Sacrament of Penance," and simply "confession."

The name "Tribunal of My mercy" is fascinating. Tribunal is the Latin term used for the three judges who presided in Roman courts. But in this Sacrament, the Three Persons of the Most Holy Trinity are the three judges: the Father, who is "rich in mercy" (Eph 2:4); the Son, who is Divine Mercy Incarnate; and the Holy Spirit, "who is "mercy in person in a transcendent way" (John Paul II, encyclical on the Holy Spirit). With such a tribunal of mercy, we have nothing to fear but unrepentant sin.

It's also interesting that in the *Diary,* Jesus describes the Sacrament of Reconciliation as the place **where the greatest miracles take place** [and] **are incessantly repeated.** Jesus goes on to point out that you don't have to go on a great pilgrimage to receive His mercy. No, all you need to do is come with faith to the feet of His representative, reveal your misery, and repent of your sins. Then **the miracle of Divine Mercy** can restore **the soul in full**, Jesus says (*Diary,* 1448).

May these entries inspire all of us to take advantage of this Great Sacrament of Mercy.

Be Not Afraid

Today I heard these words: **Pray for souls that they be not afraid to approach the tribunal of My mercy. Do not grow weary of praying for sinners. You know what a burden their souls are to My Heart. Relieve My deathly sorrow; dispense My mercy** (*Diary*, 975).

My Prayer Response:

Merciful Lord, bless souls that fear to approach the Sacrament of Reconciliation that you call the "Tribunal of My Mercy." Bless fearful souls with Your love, peace, and joy when going to receive Your mercy in confession.

A Cause of Murmuring

My daughter, I have something to tell you. I replied, "Speak, Jesus, for I thirst for Your words." **It displeases Me that, because the sisters were murmuring, you did not ask to have Father Andrasz hear your confession in your cell. Know that, because of this, you gave them even greater cause for murmuring.** Very humbly I begged the Lord's forgiveness. O my Master, rebuke me; do not overlook my faults, and do not let me err (*Diary*, 1460).

My Prayer Response:

Lord, help me not to be a cause of murmuring among my family and friends nor react to their murmuring. May I avoid offending You and be quick to beg Your forgiveness when I sin.

Do Not Put off Confession

I feel much better today. I was glad I would be able to meditate more during the Holy Hour. Then I heard a voice: **You will not be in good health. Do not put off the Sacrament of Penance, because this displeases Me. Pay little attention to the murmurs of those around you.** This surprised me, because I am feeling better today, but I gave it no more thought. When the sister switched off the light, I began the Holy Hour. But after a while something went wrong with my heart. I suffered in silence until eleven o'clock, but then I began to feel so bad that I woke up Sister N. [probably Sister Fabiola], who is my roommate, and she gave me some drops, which brought me a little relief so that I could lie down. I now understand the Lord's warning. I decided to call any priest at all, the next day, and to open the secrets of my soul to him (*Diary,* 1464).

My Prayer Response:

Lord, when You warn me not to put off the Sacrament of Penance, help me to search out a priest to hear my confession soon.

The Miracle of Divine Mercy

Write, speak of My mercy. Tell souls where they are to look for solace; that is, in the Tribunal of Mercy [the Sacrament of Reconciliation] **There the greatest miracles take place** [and] **are incessantly repeated. To avail oneself of this miracle, it is not necessary to go on a great pilgrimage or to carry out some external ceremony; it suffices to come with faith to the feet of My representative and to reveal to him one's misery, and the miracle of Divine Mercy will be fully demonstrated** (*Diary,* 1448).

My Prayer Response:

Thank You, Lord Jesus, for teaching us where to find consolation. Thank You for the Tribunal of Mercy where great miracles take place when we reveal our miseries.

Restoring the Soul in Full

Were a soul like a decaying corpse so that from a human standpoint, there would be no [hope of] **restoration and everything would already be lost, it is not so with God. The miracle of Divine Mercy restores that soul in full. Oh, how miserable are those who do not take advantage of the miracle of God's mercy! You will call out in vain, but it will be too late** (*Diary*, 1448).

My Prayer Response:

Lord Jesus, thank You for restoring souls in full by the miracle of Your mercy. May I always take advantage of it in my need.

The Blood and Water

Today the Lord said to me, **Daughter, when you go to confession, to this fountain of My mercy, the Blood and Water which came forth from My Heart always flows down upon your soul and ennobles it. Every time you go to confession, immerse yourself entirely in My mercy, with great trust, so that I may pour the bounty of My grace upon your soul. When you approach the confessional, know this, that I Myself am waiting there for you. I am only hidden by the priest, but I Myself act in your soul** (*Diary*, 1602).

My Prayer Response:

Thank You, Lord Jesus, for the Blood and Water which gushed forth from Your Heart as a fountain of mercy for me. As I approach You in confession, I immerse myself in Your mercy with great trust.

My Misery Meets Your Mercy

Here the misery of the soul meets the God of mercy. Tell souls that from this fount of mercy souls draw graces solely with the vessel of trust. If their trust is great, there is no limit to My generosity. The torrents of grace inundate humble souls. The proud remain always in poverty and misery, because My grace turns away from them to humble souls (*Diary,* 1602).

My Prayer Response:

Thank You, Lord, for confession, where my misery meets Your mercy. Help me to draw mercy from this fount of mercy with the greatest trust: "Jesus, I trust in You!"

Only a Screen

Today, the Lord has been teaching me, once again, how I am to approach the Sacrament of Penance: **My daughter, just as you prepare in My presence, so also you make your confession before Me. The person of the priest is, for Me, only a screen. Never analyze what sort of a priest it is that I am making use of; open your soul in confession as you would to Me, and I will fill it with My light** (*Diary,* 1725).

My Prayer Response:

Thank You, Lord, for teaching St. Faustina how to make her confession before You. Help me to remember that the priest is only a screen. May I, too, make my confession before You, opening my soul to You that You may fill it with Your light.

This Small Imperfection

It so happened that I fell again into a certain error, in spite of a sincere resolution not to do so — even though the lapse was a minor imperfection and rather involuntary — and at this I felt such acute pain in my soul that I interrupted my work and went to the chapel for a while. Falling at the feet of Jesus, with love and a great deal of pain, I apologized to the Lord, all the more ashamed because of the fact that in my conversation with Him after Holy Communion this very morning I had promised to be faithful to Him. Then I heard these words: **If it hadn't been for this small imperfection, you wouldn't have come to Me** (*Diary*, 1293).

My Prayer Response:

Help me, Lord Jesus, to humble myself in confession and ask for forgiveness, even for imperfections that they, too, may vanish. May I bring even the smallest imperfection to You.

An Abundance of Graces

Know that as often as you come to Me, humbling yourself and asking My forgiveness, I pour out a superabundance of graces on your soul, and your imperfection vanishes before My eyes, and I see only your love and your humility. You lose nothing but gain much … (*Diary,* 1293).

My Prayer Response:

Lord Jesus, I want to receive an abundance of Your graces in confession as I humble myself and ask for forgiveness. Thank You, Jesus, for seeing only my love and humility.

Jesus the Teacher

September 3 – 29

As I was gathering the words of Jesus to St. Faustina, I found a growing number of themes with only a few entries. Fortunately, I found a common theme among all these entries that delighted me, because I could group them under the present title of "Jesus the Teacher."

What delighted me most was to realize that Jesus is not only a divine teacher but He also gives us the grace and strength to carry out His teaching. Consider Jesus' teaching, for instance, to St. Faustina about being like a little child by trusting in Him alone:

> **Yes, I will be with you always, if you always remain a little child and fear nothing. As I was your beginning here, so I will also be your end. Do not rely on creatures, even in the smallest things, because this displeases Me. I want to be alone in your soul. I want to give light and strength to your soul, and you will learn from My representative that I am in you, and your uncertainty will vanish like mist before the rays of the sun** (*Diary*, 295).

In going through these entries, I recalled how often in the Gospels, Jesus taught His disciples and the people. In fact, there is a particular Gospel passage along these lines that captures well Jesus' role in teaching us many things, because of our great need for Him:

> When [Jesus] disembarked and saw the vast crowd, His heart was moved with pity for them, for they were like sheep without a

> shepherd; and He began to teach them many things (Mk 6:34).

As we use these entries for daily prayer and meditation, may we sit at the feet of the Master and listen to Him, for His word gives life to our souls.

Strength for the Task at Hand

One time during the novitiate, … I was very upset because I could not manage the pots, which were very large. The most difficult task for me was draining the potatoes, and sometimes I spilt half of them with the water … . I complained to God about my weakness. Then I heard the following words in my soul, **From today on you will do this easily; I shall strengthen you.**

That evening, when the time came to drain off the water from the potatoes, I hurried to be the first to do it, trusting in the Lord's words. I took up the pot with ease and poured off the water perfectly. But when I took off the cover to let the potatoes steam off, I saw there in the pot, in the place of the potatoes, whole bunches of red roses, beautiful beyond description … . [Then] I heard a voice within saying, **I change such hard work of yours into bouquets of most beautiful flowers, and their perfume rises up to My throne** (*Diary*, 65).

My Prayer Response:

Lord Jesus, when the work before me is overwhelming thank You for teaching me through St. Faustina that You give me the strength needed for the task.

The Essence of Your Lordship

On Friday, after Holy Communion, I was carried in spirit before the throne of God. There I saw the heavenly Powers which incessantly praise God. Beyond the throne I saw a brightness inaccessible to creatures, and there only the Incarnate Word enters as Mediator. When Jesus entered this light, I heard these words, **Write down at once what you hear: I am the Lord in My essence and am immune to orders or needs. If I call creatures into being — that is the abyss of My mercy.** And at that very moment I found myself, as before, in our chapel at my kneeler, just as Mass had ended. I already had these words written (*Diary,* 85).

My Prayer Response:

Thank You, Lord Jesus, for teaching St. Faustina about the essence of Your Lordship and the abyss of Your mercy in creating us. May these mysteries at the Throne of God evoke my praise and worship.

All the Graces I Can Carry

Once the Lord said to me, **Act like a beggar who does not back away when he gets more alms [than he asked for], but offers thanks the more fervently. You too, should not back away and say that you are not worthy of receiving greater graces when I give them to you. I know you are unworthy, but rejoice all the more and take as many treasures from My Heart as you can carry, for then you will please Me more** (*Diary*, 294).

My Prayer Response:

Jesus, thank You for teaching me to receive all the graces You offer me with fervent thanksgiving. Knowing that I am unworthy, I rejoice all the more and take all I can carry — to please You!

Take Graces for Others

And I will tell you one more thing — take these graces not only for yourself, but also for others; that is, encourage the souls with whom you come in contact to trust in My infinite mercy. Oh, how I love those souls who have complete confidence in Me — I will do everything for them (*Diary*, 294).

My Prayer Response:

Yes, Lord, I take Your graces not only for myself but for souls I meet that they may trust in you even more. May they grow to have complete confidence in You!

Remain a Little Child

At that moment Jesus asked me, **My child, how is your retreat going?** I answered, "But, Jesus, You know how it is going." **Yes, I know, but I want to hear it from your own lips and from your heart.** "O my Master, when You are leading me, everything goes smoothly, and I ask You, Lord, to never leave my side." And Jesus said, **Yes, I will be with you always, if you always remain a little child and fear nothing. As I was your beginning here, so I will also be your end. Do not rely on creatures, even in the smallest things, because this displeases Me. I want to be alone in your soul. I will give light and strength to your soul, and you will learn from My representative that I am in you, and your uncertainty will vanish like mist before the rays of the sun** (*Diary,* 295).

My Prayer Response:

Lord Jesus, give me the light and strength to rely on You as a little child, without fear. May I rely on You even for the smallest things, so I may please You.

Jesus Is My Director

One day, during the morning meditation, I heard this voice: **I Myself am your Director; I was, I am, and I will be. And since you asked for visible help, I chose and gave you a director even before you had asked, for My work required this. Know that the faults you commit against him wound My Heart. Be especially on your guard against self-willfulness; even the smallest thing should bear the seal of obedience.**

With a crushed and humbled heart, I begged forgiveness of Jesus for these faults. I also begged pardon of my spiritual director and resolved to do nothing rather than to do many things wrongly (*Diary*, 362).

My Prayer Response:

Lord Jesus, thank You for being my Director and Teacher. I also ask You to give me help through a visible director to guide me according to Your will and not mine.

The Generosity of Jesus

Once, the Lord said to me, **My daughter, take the graces that others spurn; take as many as you can carry.** At that moment, my soul was inundated with the love of God. I feel that I am united with the Lord so closely that I cannot find words to express that union; in this state I suddenly feel that all the things God has, all the goods and treasures, are mine, although I set little store by them, for He alone is enough for me. In Him I see my everything; without Him — nothing (*Diary*, 454).

December 18, [1936]. Today I felt bad that a week had gone by and no one had come to visit me. When I complained to the Lord, He answered, **Isn't it enough for you that I visit you every day?** I apologized to the Lord and the hurt vanished. O God, my strength, You are sufficient for me (*Diary*, 827).

My Prayer Response:

Lord Jesus, what a blessing to read of Your generosity to a soul like that of St. Faustina. I sure could use some of those graces that others spurn. Lavish me with Your graces, Lord.

Love Keeps Jesus with Us

O Holy Trinity, Eternal God, my spirit is drowned in Your beauty. The ages are as nothing in Your sight. You are always the same. Oh, how great is Your majesty. Jesus, why do You conceal Your majesty, why have You left Your heavenly throne and dwelt among us? The Lord answered me, **My daughter, love has brought Me here, and love keeps Me here. My daughter, if you knew what great merit and reward is earned by one act of pure love for Me, you would die of joy** (*Diary*, 576).

My Prayer Response:

Lord Jesus, what great love has brought You to dwell in our earth! Teach me how to act with a pure love for You. Thank You for loving me.

Unite Yourself to Jesus

I am saying this that you may constantly unite yourself with Me through love, for this is the goal of the life of your soul. This act is an act of the will. Know that a pure soul is humble. When you lower and empty yourself before My majesty, I then pursue you with My graces and make use of My omnipotence to exalt you (*Diary*, 576).

My Prayer Response:

Lord Jesus, I want to love You and constantly unite myself to You. Teach me how to lower and empty myself before Your Majesty. Keep my soul pure and humble before You.

Jesus Wants to Teach Us

When once I felt hurt because of a certain thing and complained to the Lord, Jesus answered, **My daughter, why do you attach such importance to the teaching and the talk of people? I Myself want to teach you; that is why I arrange things so that you cannot attend those conferences. In a single moment, I will bring you to know more than others will acquire through many years of toil** (*Diary*, 1147).

My Prayer Response:

Jesus, please be my teacher! Teach me to know and love You and so serve You better. I know that You Yourself want to teach me. Give me ears to hear You.

God's Mercy Time and Again

As I was meditating on the sin of the Angels and their immediate punishment, I asked Jesus why the Angels had been punished as soon as they had sinned. I heard a voice: **Because of their profound knowledge of God. No person on earth, even though a great saint, has such knowledge of God as an Angel has.** Nevertheless, to me who am so miserable, You have shown Your mercy, O God, and this, time and time again. You carry me in the bosom of Your mercy and forgive me every time that I ask Your forgiveness with a contrite heart (*Diary,* 1332).

My Prayer Response:

Lord Jesus, please help me to know You and Your greatest attribute, Your mercy. Help me to tell Your people of Your compassion and love. As I do, also give me courage to ask Your forgiveness whenever I sin.

Let Go of Yourself

During Holy Hour today, I asked the Lord Jesus if He would deign to teach me about the spiritual life, Jesus answered me, **My daughter, faithfully live up to the words which I speak to you. Do not value any external thing too highly, even if it were to seem very precious to you. Let go of yourself, and abide with Me continually** (*Diary*, 1685).

My Prayer Response:

Lord Jesus, as You taught St. Faustina about the spiritual life, teach me, too, that I might "let go of myself and abide with You continually."

Do Nothing on Your Own

Entrust everything to Me and do nothing on your own, and you will always have great freedom of spirit. No circumstances or events will ever be able to upset you. Set little store on what people say. Let everyone judge you as they like. Do not make excuses for yourself, it will do you no harm (*Diary,* 1685).

My Prayer Response:

Lord Jesus, help me to entrust every thing to You and do nothing on my own, so I will always have great freedom of spirit.

Give Away Everything

Give away everything at the first sign of a demand, even if they were the most necessary things. Do not ask for anything without consulting Me. Allow them to take away even what is due you — respect, your good name — let your spirit rise above all that. And so, set free from everything, rest close to My Heart, not allowing your peace to be disturbed by anything. My pupil, consider the words which I have spoken to you (*Diary*, 1685).

My Prayer Response:

Lord Jesus, what a marvelous freedom You taught St. Faustina: to give away everything at the first sign of a demand. Teach me what I need to do to have such a free spirit.

The Treasure of Grace

Today I saw the Crucified Lord Jesus. Precious pearls and diamonds were pouring forth from the wound in His Heart. I saw how a multitude of souls was gathering these gifts, but there was one soul who was closest to His Heart and she, knowing the greatness of these gifts, was gathering them with liberality, not only for herself, but for others as well. The Savior said to me, **Behold, the treasures of grace that flow down upon souls, but not all souls know how to take advantage of My generosity** (*Diary,* 1687).

My Prayer Response:

Thank You, Jesus, for teaching us through St. Faustina that Your graces flow like "precious pearls and diamonds" from the wound in Your Heart. Teach us how to take advantage of Your generosity and gather Your graces for ourselves and for others.

Great Calm and Patience

I asked the Lord today that He might deign to teach me about the interior life, because of myself I can neither understand nor conceive anything perfectly. The Lord answered me, **I was your Teacher, I am and I will be; strive to make your heart like unto My humble and gentle Heart. Never claim your rights. Bear with great calm and patience everything that befalls you** (*Diary*, 1701).

My Prayer Response:

Lord Jesus, teach me about the interior life. Help me to make my heart like Your humble and gentle Heart. May I be calm and patient with everything that comes my way.

Thankful for Everything

Do not defend yourself when you are put to shame, though innocent. Let others triumph. Do not stop being good when you notice that your goodness is being abused. I Myself will speak up for you when it is necessary. Be grateful for the smallest of My graces, because your gratitude compels Me to grant you new graces … (*Diary*, 1701).

My Prayer Response:

Lord Jesus, help me not to defend myself when put to shame. May I be thankful for everything, especially for the smallest of Your graces.

Part One of Conference

Conference on Sacrifice and Prayer.

My daughter, I want to instruct you on how you are to rescue souls through sacrifice and prayer. You will save more souls through prayer and suffering than will a missionary through his teachings and sermons alone. I want to see you as a sacrifice of living love, which only then carries weight before Me (*Diary*, 1767).

My Prayer Response:

Lord Jesus, thank You for Your teaching on sacrifice and prayer. By my prayer and suffering with love, may I help save souls. Make me a spiritual missionary of Your mercy.

Part Two of Conference

Conference on Sacrifice and Prayer.

You must be annihilated, destroyed, living as if you were dead in the most secret depths of your being. You must be destroyed in that secret depth where the human eye has never penetrated; then will I find in you a pleasing sacrifice, a holocaust full of sweetness and fragrance. And great will be your power for whomever you intercede (*Diary,* 1767).

My Prayer Response:

Lord Jesus, help me surrender to the depth of my being to You. I want to cross out my self-will like St. Faustina did (see *Diary*, 374) with a big X and do Your will as a living sacrifice pleasing to You (see Rom 12:1).

Part Three of Conference

Conference on Sacrifice and Prayer.

Outwardly, your sacrifice must look like this: silent, hidden, permeated with love, imbued with prayer. I demand, My daughter, that your sacrifice be pure and full of humility, that I may find pleasure in it. I will not spare My grace, that you may be able to fulfill what I demand of you (*Diary,* 1767).

My Prayer Response:

Lord Jesus, may my sacrifice be silent, hidden, loving, prayerful, and joyful! May it be pure and humble, so it may please You. Fulfill Your purpose for my life.

Part Four of Conference

Conference on Sacrifice and Prayer.

I will now instruct you on what your holocaust shall consist of, in everyday life, so as to preserve you from illusions. You shall accept all sufferings with love. Do not be afflicted if your heart often experiences repugnance and dislike for sacrifice (*Diary,* 1767).

My Prayer Response:

Lord Jesus, by Your grace and with Your love that You showed me on the Cross, may I accept all sufferings with love. May I come to know like St. Faustina that suffering plus love equals joy!

Part Five of Conference

Conference on Sacrifice and Prayer.

All its power rests in the will, and so these contrary feelings, far from lowering the value of the sacrifice in My eyes, will enhance it. Know that your body and soul will often be in the midst of fire. Although you will not feel My presence on some occasions, I will always be with you. Do not fear; My grace will be with you ... (*Diary*, 1767).

My Prayer Response:

Lord Jesus, in the midst of suffering, may I hear the words of Your promise: **I will always be with you. Do not fear; My grace will be with you.**

Part One of Conference

Conference on Mercy.

My daughter, know that My Heart is mercy itself. From this sea of mercy, graces flow out upon the whole world. No soul that has approached Me has ever gone away unconsoled. All misery gets buried in the depths of My mercy, and every saving and sanctifying grace flows from this fountain (*Diary*, 1777).

My Prayer Response:

Thank, You Jesus, for this *five-star teaching* on Your mercy! Thank You for Your Heart, which is mercy itself, a sea of mercy, a fountain of mercy from which flows **every saving and sanctifying grace**! May I and all who approach You be immersed in the sea of Your mercy.

Part Two of Conference

Conference on Mercy.

My daughter, I desire that your heart be an abiding place of My mercy. I desire that this mercy flow out upon the whole world through your heart. Let no one who approaches you go away without that trust in My mercy which I so ardently desire for souls (*Diary*, 1777).

My Prayer Response:

Lord Jesus, may Your desires for St. Faustina, be fulfilled in me as well. I, too, desire that my heart be an abiding place of Your mercy, so it may flow out to the whole world and souls may learn to trust in You!

Part Three of Conference

Conference on Mercy.

Pray as much as you can for the dying. By your entreaties, obtain for them trust in My mercy, because they have most need of trust, and have it the least. Be assured that the grace of eternal salvation for certain souls in their final moment depends on your prayer (*Diary,* 1777).

You know the whole abyss of My mercy, so draw upon it for yourself and especially for poor sinners. Sooner would heaven and earth turn into nothingness than would My mercy not embrace a trusting soul (*Diary,* 1777).

My Prayer Response:

Lord Jesus, teach me how to pray for the dying. May I obtain for them the grace of trust in Your mercy in their final moments: "Jesus, I trust in You!"

Lord Jesus, may I teach poor sinners to trust in You. And may all of us; *"Trust in Jesus even more!"*

If Only

Today, in the course of a long conversation, the Lord said to me, **How very much I desire the salvation of souls! My dearest secretary, write that I want to pour out My divine life into human souls and sanctify them, if only they were willing to accept My grace. The greatest sinners would achieve great sanctity, if only they would trust in My mercy** (*Diary,* 1784).

My Prayer Response:

O Lord Jesus, what power is in the two words: "if only." You want to sanctity me and all souls *if only* we were willing to accept Your grace — *if only* we would trust in Your mercy!

The Spiritual Guide of Souls

The very inner depths of My being are filled to overflowing with mercy, and it is being poured out upon all I have created. My delight is to act in a human soul and to fill it with My mercy and to justify it. My kingdom on earth is My life in the human soul. Write, My secretary, that I Myself am the spiritual guide of souls — and I guide them indirectly through the priest, and lead each one to sanctity by a road known to Me alone (*Diary*, 1784).

My Prayer Response:

Lord Jesus, fulfill Your delight and fill souls that trust in You with Your mercy. Guide each one of us to sanctity by a road known to You alone. You are the spiritual guide of my soul.

Union of Love

September 30 – October 10

As was the case with St. Faustina and the Lord Jesus, the union between God and a soul is a transforming love that is unique in its expression. This union of love is described by St. Faustina:

> Intimate communion of a soul with God. God approaches a soul in a *special* way known only to Himself and to the soul. No one perceives this mysterious union. Love presides in this union, and everything is achieved by love alone (*Diary*, 622, emphasis added).

Now the original text of the *Diary* is in Polish, and the word "special" in Polish is opposite to the word for "universal." So the translation for the word "special" could be unique, singular, particular, individual, or exceptional. Using the word "singular" in English would then clarify some of the *Diary* entries where our Lord speaks to St. Faustina about their union of love:

> **That is why I am uniting Myself with you so intimately as with no other creature** (*Diary*, 707).
>
> **I unite Myself with you more closely than with any other creature …** (*Diary*, 1546).
>
> **… it is solely out of mercy that I grant you the grace of union with Myself** (*Diary*, 1576).
>
> **My gaze rests kindly upon you before any other creature** (*Diary*, 1700).

What we find in these entries describing the exceptional union of the Lord with St. Faustina is an example of the "special and singular" union of love that God calls each of us to experience now and in eternity. God's plan for us is to form the family of His children, created in His image and likeness. And yet each member of the family of God is a unique, precious, and unrepeatable image of God.

As you read these entries and respond in prayer, consider what this important truth could mean to your special relationship with the Lord Jesus.

In the Smallest Things

At the chapter, Mother [Borgia] stressed a life of faith and fidelity in small things. Half way through the chapter, I heard these words: **I desire that you would all have more faith at the present time. How great is My joy at the faithfulness of My spouse in the smallest things.** Then I looked at the crucifix and saw that Jesus' head was turned towards the refectory, and His lips were moving (*Diary*, 352).

My Prayer Response:

Dearest Jesus, I desire to be more faithful to You even in the smallest things in my daily life. I desire and long to live in union with You and be the joy of Your Heart.

The Call to Intimacy

I heard these words in my soul: **You are My spouse forever; your chastity should be greater than that of the angels, for I call no angel to such intimacy as I do you. The smallest act of My spouse is of infinite value. A pure soul has inconceivable power before God** (*Diary*, 534).

My Prayer Response:

Lord Jesus, thank You for the call to intimacy with You in a chaste union of love. Purify my heart, O Lord! May I make use of Your merciful love for me to intercede for the salvation of souls.

You Alone, Lord

Once, I suddenly saw Jesus in great majesty, and He spoke these words to me: **My daughter, if you wish, I will this instant create a new world, more beautiful than this one, and you will live there for the rest of your life.** I answered, "I don't want any worlds. I want You, Jesus. I want to love You, with the same love that You have for me. I beg You for only one thing: to make my heart capable of loving You. I am very much surprised at Your offer, my Jesus; what are those worlds to me? Even if You gave me a thousand of them, what are they to me? You know very well, Jesus, that my heart is dying of longing for You. Everything that is not You is nothing to me." … Then I heard these words: **With no other soul do I unite Myself as closely and in such a way as I do with you, and this because of the deep humility and ardent love which you have for Me** (*Diary*, 587).

My Prayer Response:

Dearest Jesus, like St. Faustina, I want to desire only You. I want to live now and in eternity with humble obedience to Your will — out of a love that is on fire for You alone.

A Pure Victim of Love

October 2, 1936. The First Friday of the month. After Holy Communion, I suddenly saw the Lord Jesus, who spoke these words to me: **Now I know that it is not for the graces or gifts that you love Me, but because My will is dearer to you than life. That is why I am uniting Myself with you so intimately as with no other creature** (*Diary,* 707).

When I entered the chapel for a five-minute adoration, I asked the Lord Jesus how I should conduct myself during this retreat. Then I heard this voice in my soul: **I desire that you be entirely transformed into love and that you burn ardently as a pure victim of love ...** (*Diary,* 726).

My Prayer Response:

Lord Jesus, You know my miseries and weaknesses better than I do, but Your infinite mercy can set my heart on fire for You alone. Make me burn ardently as a pure victim of love. Have mercy on me, a sinner, and on the whole world!

Gratitude for God's Mercy

In the evening, a great longing took possession of my soul. I took the pamphlet with the Image of the Merciful Jesus on it and pressed it to my heart, and the following words burst forth from my soul: "Jesus, Eternal Love, I live for You, I die for You, and I want to become united with You." Suddenly, I saw the Lord in His inexpressible beauty. He looked at me graciously and said, **My daughter, I too came down from heaven out of love for you; I lived for you, I died for you, and I created the heavens for you.** And Jesus pressed me to His Heart and said to me, **Very soon now; be at peace, My daughter.** When I was alone, my soul was set afire with the desire to suffer until the moment when the Lord would say, "Enough" (*Diary,* 853).

My Prayer Response:

Lord Jesus, thank You for what You have done for me and for the whole world. I thank You for the love You have for me. I also thank You for the love and mercy You want to pour out on all mankind. I thank You even for those who have not thanked You. Give them grateful hearts, O Lord.

Fill Me, Lord

Then I heard the following words spoken thus: **I want you to be My spouse.** Fear pierced my soul, but I calmly continued to reflect on what sort of an espousal this could be. However, each time fear would invade my soul, a power from on high would give it peace (*Diary*, 912).

The Lord said to me, **I want to give Myself to souls and to fill them with My love, but few there are who want to accept all the graces My love has intended for them. My grace is not lost; if the soul for whom it was intended does not accept it, another soul takes it** (*Diary*, 1017).

My Prayer Response:

Lord Jesus, You want to give Yourself to souls and fill them with Your love and mercy. But so many souls refuse Your love. Change my heart, Lord, to desire You alone. And fill me with Your love and mercy.

By Your Will, Lord

Today, I received some oranges. When the sister had left, I thought to myself, "Should I eat the oranges instead of doing penance and mortifying myself during Holy Lent? After all, I am feeling a bit better." Then I heard a voice in my soul: **My daughter, you please Me more by eating the oranges out of obedience and love of Me than by fasting and mortifying yourself of your own will. A soul that loves Me very much must, ought to live by My will. I know your heart, and I know that it will not be satisfied by anything but My love alone** (*Diary,* 1023).

My Prayer Response:

Lord Jesus, help me to love You even more and live by Your will. Teach me to unite even my smallest deeds with You and so please our heavenly Father.

As Your Own

Today toward evening, the Lord said to me, **Entrust yourself completely to Me at the hour of death, and I will present you to My Father as My bride. And now I recommend that you unite, in a special way, even your smallest deeds to My merits, and then My Father will look upon them with love as if they were My own** (*Diary*, 1543).

My Prayer Response:

Lord Jesus, I entrust myself to You at the hour of my death. May I be completely united to You in love at that hour. Present me to the Father with love as Your own.

With Freshness of Heart

The Lord said to me, **I am delighted with your love. Your sincere love is as pleasing to My Heart as the fragrance of a rosebud at morningtide, before the sun has taken the dew from it. The freshness of your heart captivates Me; that is why I unite Myself with you more closely than with any other creature …** (*Diary*, 1546).

Then I heard the words: **As you are united with Me in life, so will you be united at the moment of death.** After these words, such great trust in God's great mercy was awakened in my soul that, even if I had had the sins of the whole world, as well as the sins of all the condemned souls weighing on my conscience, I would not have doubted God's goodness but, without hesitation, would have thrown myself into the abyss of the divine mercy, which is always open to us … (*Diary*, 1552).

My Prayer Response:

Lord Jesus, help me to love You with freshness of heart that will delight You. Help me to abandon myself totally to Your holy will, which is mercy itself. Let me never doubt Your great mercy.

Solely out of Mercy

Know, My daughter, that between Me and you there is a bottomless abyss, an abyss which separates the Creator from the creature. But this abyss is filled with My mercy. I raise you up to Myself, not that I have need of you, but it is solely out of mercy that I grant you the grace of union with Myself (*Diary*, 1576).

My Prayer Response:

My Lord Jesus, fill in the bottomless abyss that separates You from me. Fill in the chasm with Your unfathomable mercy. Lord, the whole world needs Your kind of mercy now. Come, Lord Jesus, and please hurry up!

United with You Forever

This evening, the Lord asked me, **Do you not have any desires in your heart?** I answered, "I have one great desire, and it is to be united with You forever." And the Lord answered me, **That will happen soon. My dearest child, your every stirring is reflected in My Heart. My gaze rests kindly upon you before any other creature** (*Diary*, 1700).

My Prayer Response:

Lord Jesus, the desire of my heart is to have the one great desire of St. Faustina: "to be united with You forever." May I grow in that desire by Your loving mercy and grace.

Writing

October 11 – 18

It is amazing to me that St. Faustina wrote a *Diary* of more than 600 pages with so little free time, because of her convent duties and prayer time. The Lord provided extra time during her stays in the sanatorium to treat her tuberculosis and when she was assigned as a doorkeeper.

But even more amazing is what she was able to write with only three semesters of elementary schooling. Cardinal Andrew Deskur, a classmate of Karol Wojtyla in the seminary, introduced the future Pope John Paul II to The Divine Mercy teachings of Sr. Faustina. In his preface to the original Polish edition of the *Diary*, Cardinal Deskur described the saint and her writing in this way:

> The reader, after just a superficial skimming of the *Diary*, may be struck by the simplicity of the language and even by the spelling and stylistic errors, but he should never forget that the author of the *Diary* had but a limited elementary education. The theology alone which is found in the *Diary* awakens in the reader a conviction of its uniqueness; and if one considers the contrast between [Saint] Faustina's education and the loftiness of her theology, the contrast alone indicates the special influence of Divine Grace.

Sister Faustina wrote her *Diary* in obedience to her spiritual director, Fr. Michael Sopocko. The Lord directed her what to write about His mercy. The words of the Lord in this section show the Lord's concern that she **devote all** [her] **free moments to writing it** (*Diary*, 1693).

By an interior light from the Lord, St. Faustina learned that not a single word was hers. She always fulfilled God's will as He made it known to her (see *Diary*, 1667).

Writing the *Diary* was an important part of St. Faustina's call as the great Apostle of Divine Mercy. We should be grateful for this precious gift that she left the Church and our troubled world!

Along with gratitude for this gift, we should each ask ourselves: How is the Lord calling me to spread the message of Divine Mercy?

For the Benefit of Souls

You have not written everything in the notebook about My goodness towards humankind; I desire that you omit nothing; I desire that your heart be firmly grounded in total peace (*Diary,* 459).

January 23, [1937]. I did not feel like writing today. Then I heard a voice in my soul: **My daughter, you do not live for yourself but for souls; write for their benefit. You know that My will as to your writing has been confirmed many times by your confessors. You know what is pleasing to Me, and if you have any doubts about what I am saying, you also know whom you are to ask. I grant him light to pronounce judgment on my case. My eye watches over him. My daughter, you are to be like a child towards him, full of simplicity and candor. Put his judgment above all My demands. He will guide you according to My will** (*Diary,* 895).

My Prayer Response:

Lord Jesus, thank You for making known to St. Faustina the importance of writing her *Diary*. Thank You for stressing to her that she was to live and write for the benefit of souls like ourselves.

Underlining Jesus' Words

When I set to work at underlining the Lord's words and thus was going through everything in sequence, I reached the page where I had marked down Father Andrasz's advice and directions. I did not know what to do, to underline or not to underline, and then I heard these words in my soul: **Underline, because these words are Mine; I have borrowed the lips of the friend of My Heart in order to speak to you and reassure you. You are to observe these directions until your death. It would not please Me at all if you were to disobey these directions. Know that it is I who have placed him between Myself and your soul. I am doing this to set you at peace and so that you may not err** (*Diary*, 967).

My Prayer Response:

Thank You, Lord Jesus, that You inspired Fr. Andrasz to have Sr. Faustina underline Your words in her *Diary*. Underlining them, now printing them in boldface, made it easier to gather Your words in this daily devotional — all for our spiritual benefit.

Your Ocean of Mercy

My daughter, be diligent in writing down every sentence I tell you concerning My mercy, because this is meant for a great number of souls who will profit from it (*Diary*, 1142).

Jesus: **My daughter, do you think you have written enough about My mercy? What you have written is but a drop compared to the ocean. I am Love and Mercy Itself. There is no misery that could be a match for My mercy, neither will misery exhaust it, because as it is being granted — it increases. The soul that trusts in My mercy is most fortunate, because I Myself take care of it** (*Diary*, 1273).

My Prayer Response:

What a gift You have prepared for us readers in the *Diary of St. Faustina*. Thank You for Your encouragement to St. Faustina to keep on writing, especially about Your ocean of mercy toward the miserable.

Only a Single Drop

My Secretary, write that I am more generous toward sinners than toward the just. It was for their sake that I came down from heaven; it was for their sake that My Blood was spilled. Let them not fear to approach Me; they are most in need of My mercy (*Diary,* 1275).

During Holy Hour in the evening, I heard the words, **You see My mercy for sinners, which at this moment is revealing itself in all its power. See how little you have written about it; it is only a single drop. Do what is in your power, so that sinners may come to know My goodness** (*Diary,* 1665).

My Prayer Response:

Thank You, Lord Jesus, for Your exceptional love for sinners. May we sinners take full advantage of the mercy You described to St. Faustina. May we come to know Your goodness.

Bless This Pen

As I took the pen in hand, I addressed a short prayer to the Holy Spirit and said, "Jesus, bless this pen so that everything You order me to write may be for the glory of God." Then I heard a voice: **Yes, I bless** [it], **because this writing bears the seal of obedience to your superior and confessor, and by that very fact I am already given glory, and many souls will be drawing profit from it. My daughter, I demand that you devote all your free moments to writing about My goodness and mercy. It is your office and your assignment throughout your life to continue to make known to souls the great mercy I have for them and to exhort them to trust in My bottomless mercy** (*Diary,* 1567).

My Prayer Response:

Thank You, Lord Jesus, for blessing the pen of St. Faustina with which she wrote under holy obedience. Her faithfulness to You continues to inspire people around the world. Her *Diary* has now been translated into dozens of languages and reaches out to millions in need of Your mercy.

Secretary of My Mercy

Write down everything that occurs to you regarding My goodness. I answered, "What do You mean, Lord, what if I write too much?" And the Lord replied, **My daughter, even if you were to speak at one and the same time in all human and angelic tongues, even then you would not have said very much, but on the contrary, you would have sung in only a small measure the praises of My goodness — of My unfathomable mercy.**

O my Jesus, You Yourself must put words into my mouth, that I may praise You worthily.

My daughter, be at peace; do as I tell you. Your thoughts are united to My thoughts, so write whatever comes to your mind. You are the secretary of My mercy. I have chosen you for that office in this life and the next life (*Diary,* 1605).

My Prayer Response:

Praise You, Lord Jesus, that You insisted to St. Faustina that she could never write enough about Your unfathomable mercy! Praise You, Jesus, for inspiring her.

St. Faustina's Faithfulness

Holy Saturday [April 16, 1938]. During adoration, the Lord said to me, **Be at peace, My daughter. This work of mercy is Mine; there is nothing of you in it. It pleases Me that you are carrying out faithfully what I have commanded you to do, not adding or taking away a single word.** And He gave me an interior light by which I learned that not a single word was mine; despite difficulties and adversities, I have always, always, fulfilled His will, as He has made it known to me (*Diary*, 1667).

My Prayer Response:

Lord Jesus, thank You for St. Faustina's faithfulness to writing about Your mercy, so that each word written is available to us as Your word. May we take advantage of Your gift by regularly reading her *Diary* to aid us in our spiritual life.

Jesus Arranged Things

As I was writing the above words, I saw the Lord Jesus leaning over me, and He asked, **My daughter, what are you writing?** I answered, "I am writing about You, Jesus, … about Your inconceivable love and mercy for people." And Jesus said, **Secretary of My most profound mystery, know that yours is an exclusive intimacy with Me. Your task is to write down everything that I make known to you about My mercy, for the benefit of those who by reading these things will be comforted in their souls and will have the courage to approach Me. I therefore want you to devote all your free moments to writing.** "But, O Lord, shall I always have a moment, at least a brief one, in which to write?" And Jesus answered, **It is not for you to think about that. Only do as much as you can, and I will always arrange things so that you will easily be able to do what I ask of you …** (*Diary,* 1693).

My Prayer Response:

Lord Jesus, thank You for arranging that the *Diary of St. Faustina* is available to us as a comfort and encouragement to approach You with great trust.

God's Will Vs. Our Self-Will

October 19 – 23

God created mankind with a free will, so we could choose freely to do His will and love Him. He so respects the freedom He gave us — as men and women created in His own image and likeness — that He will not violate it. He asks, urges, and expresses His fatherly desire that we surrender our will to His. Because of sin and our fallen nature, we experience tension in our daily lives between God's will and our self-will. We are especially called to seek God's will in discerning our vocation in life.

The Lord explained this tension to St. Faustina and asked her to surrender her will in a dramatic way when she was on retreat in 1935:

> **During this retreat, I will strengthen you in peace and in courage so that your strength will not fail in carrying out My designs. Therefore, you will cancel out your will absolutely in this retreat and instead, My complete will shall be accomplished in you. Know that it will cost you much, so write on a clean sheet of paper: "From today on, my own will does not exist," and then cross out the page. And on the other side write these words: "From today on, I do the will of God everywhere, always, and in everything." Be afraid of nothing; love will give you strength and make the realization of this easy** (*Diary*, 372).

Later, in her Act of Oblation in 1937, she could express her total submission to the will of God in this way: " Lead me, O God, along whatever roads You please; I have placed all my trust in Your will which is, for me, love and mercy itself" (*Diary,* 1264).

Consider God's will for your life as you read these entries and spend time in daily prayer. What do you think God's will is for your life? Listen carefully for His voice, so you can discern His will for you. In prayer, ask Him frequently, "Lord, reveal Your will to me. I want to do Your will everywhere, always, and in everything."

Mortify Your Self-Will

When I left the confessional and started to recite my penance, I heard these words: **I have granted the grace you asked for on behalf of that soul, but not because of the mortification you chose for yourself, but because of the act of complete obedience to My representative did I grant grace to that soul for whom you interceded and begged mercy. Know that when you mortify your own self-will, then Mine reigns within you** (*Diary*, 365).

My Prayer Response:

Lord Jesus, help me to mortify my own self-will, so Your will shall reign within me. Give me opportunities through such mortification to help souls in need.

Strengthened to Do God's Will

I am surprised that you still have not completely renounced your self-will, but I rejoice exceedingly that this change will be accomplished during the retreat (*Diary,* 369).

[Then] I heard these words: **I am with you. During this retreat, I will strengthen you in peace and in courage so that your strength will not fail in carrying out My designs. Therefore, you will cancel out your will absolutely in this retreat and, instead, My complete will shall be accomplished in you. Know that it will cost you much, so write these words on a clean sheet of paper: "From today on, my own will does not exist," and then cross out the page. And on the other side write these words: "From today on, I do the will of God everywhere, always, and in everything"** (*Diary,* 372).

My Prayer Response:

Lord Jesus, may Your love strengthen me to do Your will everywhere, always, and in everything. May I live the "Our Father" petition: "Thy will be done!"

What You Desire, Lord

I desire that you live according to My will, in the most secret depths of your soul. I reflected on these words, which spoke very much to my heart (*Diary,* 443).

Jesus bent toward me, looked at me kindly and spoke to me about the will of the Heavenly Father. He told me that the most perfect and holy soul is the one that does the will of My Father, but there are not many such, and that He looks with special love upon the soul who lives His will. And Jesus told me that I was doing the will of God perfectly ... **and for this reason I am uniting Myself with you and communing with you in a special and intimate way** (*Diary,* 603).

I was left alone with Jesus, and I said, "Jesus, take me now, for Your will has already been accomplished." And Jesus answered, **My will has not yet been completely accomplished in you; you will still suffer much, but I am with you; do not fear** (*Diary,* 675).

My Prayer Response:

Lord Jesus, I desire what You desire for my life. May I live Your will in the depths of my soul.

A Pleasing Sacrifice to God

During Holy Mass I prayed fervently that Jesus might become King of all hearts and that divine grace might shine in every soul. Then I saw Jesus as He is depicted in the image, and He said to me, **My daughter, you give Me the greatest glory by faithfully fulfilling My desires** (*Diary*, 500).

During my meditation, I heard these words: **My daughter, you give Me most glory by patiently submitting to My will, and you win for yourself greater merit than that which any fast or mortification could ever gain for you. Know, My daughter, that if you submit your will to Mine, you draw upon yourself My special delight. This sacrifice is pleasing to Me and full of sweetness. I take great pleasure in it; there is power in it** (*Diary*, 904).

My Prayer Response:

Lord Jesus, I want to give You the greatest glory by faithfully fulfilling Your desires and so pleasing You. Take pleasure in my sacrifice, O Lord.

Prepared for All Sacrifices

Today after Holy Communion, the Lord told me, **My daughter, My delight is to unite Myself with you. It is when you submit yourself to My will that you give Me the greatest glory and draw down upon yourself a sea of blessings. I would not take such special delight in you if you were not living by My will** (*Diary*, 954).

February 15, 1937. Today, I heard these words in my soul: **Host, pleasing to My Father, know, My daughter, that the entire Holy Trinity finds Its special delight in you, because you live exclusively by the will of God. No sacrifice can compare with this** (*Diary*, 955).

My Prayer Response with St. Faustina:

O my sweet Guest, I am prepared for all sacrifices for Your sake, but You know that I am weakness itself. Nevertheless, with You I can do all things. O my Jesus, I beseech You, be with me at each instant (*Diary*, 954).

Suffering for Souls

October 24 – November 20

The entries in this section are among the most challenging ones in the *Diary of St. Faustina,* as we come face-to-face with the mystery of suffering and try to fathom its purpose in our lives. In her *Diary,* Sr. Faustina records an extensive lesson on suffering, especially the value of offering it to the Lord for poor souls in need of His mercy. We might even consider the *Diary* as a book on how to suffer, as St. Faustina gives her own experience of suffering, both spiritual and physical, and the Lord's teaching on the role of suffering. As the Lord Jesus told her on Holy Thursday in 1934: **I desire that you make an offering of yourself for sinners and especially for those souls who have lost hope in God's mercy** (*Diary,* 308).

This call to suffer did not come easily for St. Faustina, but it brought her great joy when she suffered out of love for the Lord Jesus and for the salvation of souls. Consider this incident with one of her fellow sisters:

> Once when I was suffering greatly, I left my work and escaped to Jesus and asked Him to give me strength. After a very short prayer, I returned to my work filled with enthusiasm and joy. Then, one of the sisters [probably Sister Justine] said to me, "You must have many consolations today, Sister; you look so radiant. Surely, God is giving you no suffering, but only consolations." "You are greatly mistaken, Sister," I answered, "for it is precisely when I suffer that my joy is greater; and when

> I suffer less, my joy also is less." ... I tried to explain to her that when we suffer much we have a great chance to show God that we love Him (*Diary*, 303).

I am reminded of St. Paul's words in his letter to the Colossians: "Now I rejoice in my sufferings for your sake, and in my flesh I am filling up what is lacking in the afflictions of Christ on behalf of His body, which is the church" (1:24).

Our suffering, then, can be joyful and redemptive. It can have real value, especially for the salvation of souls. So, following the example of St. Paul, St. Faustina, and countless other saints, the real challenge becomes deciding *not to waste our sufferings.* Here, it's not a question of taking on more sufferings, Rather, it's a question of offering the suffering and miseries that we do, in fact, have to Jesus for the salvation of souls.

My prayer is that you embrace this call with joy as you reflect on these *Diary* entries. Along with remembering poor sinners, may you be inspired to pray for every soul who carries heavy burdens of suffering and misery.

A Note to the Reader: With the entries, I would encourage you to refer to the *Diary* text when you want to know the circumstances of the words of Jesus and so more clearly understand His words. I have included the surrounding circumstances of a few of the entries to help you appreciate the Lord's words.

Not Living for Ourselves

You are not living for yourself but for souls, and other souls will profit from your sufferings. Your prolonged suffering will give them the light and strength to accept My will (*Diary,* 67).

My Prayer Response:

Lord Jesus, help me and souls that are suffering with Your light and strength to accept Your will. Teach us, Lord, the value and profit of suffering for souls. Remind us that we are not living for ourselves.

Bless Souls Who Suffer

You are the delight of My Heart; from today on, every one of your acts, even the very smallest, will be a delight to My eyes, whatever you do (*Diary,* 137).

My daughter, consider these words: "And being in agony, he prayed more earnestly" (*Diary,* 157).

My Prayer Response:

Lord Jesus, when St. Faustina consented to the sacrifice You asked of her with all her heart, You blessed her (see *Diary,* 137). At that moment, she felt "extraordinarily fused with God." Jesus, please help all who are suffering to accept Your will and bless them with Your loving presence!

Pure and Unadulterated

My child, you please Me most by suffering. In your physical as well as your mental sufferings, My daughter, do not seek sympathy from creatures. I want the fragrance of your suffering to be pure and unadulterated (*Diary*, 279).

My Prayer Response:

Lord Jesus, may souls who are suffering offer their sufferings in union with Yours — like the pure and unadulterated fragrance of incense — all for souls.

Come to Love Suffering

I want you to detach yourself, not only from creatures, but also from yourself. My daughter, I want to delight in the love of your heart, a pure love, virginal, unblemished, untarnished. The more you will come to love suffering, My daughter, the purer your love for Me will be (*Diary*, 279).

My Prayer Response:

Lord Jesus, only with Your love can I come to love suffering. Love me that I may love and carry my cross daily. Help us all to be Your disciples as You taught us: "If anyone wishes to come after Me, he must deny himself and take up his cross daily and follow Me" (Lk 9:23).

Great Pain for Sin

My Heart was moved by great mercy towards you, My dearest child, when I saw you torn to shreds because of the great pain you suffered in repenting for your sins (*Diary*, 282).

My Prayer Response:

Lord Jesus, You promised to St. Faustina that the sinner has the greatest right to Your mercy (see *Diary*, 723, 1146, 1275). Have mercy, Lord, on all who strive to repent and reform.

Lift Us up

I see your love, so pure and true that I give you first place among the virgins. You are the honor and glory of My Passion. I see every abasement of your soul, and nothing escapes my attention. I lift up the humble even to My very throne, because I want it so (*Diary*, 282).

My Prayer Response:

Lord Jesus, through the intercession of St. Faustina, help us to humble ourselves in our sufferings and lift us up to Your throne. Let us see Your glory, Lord, even in the midst of our sufferings.

Undeserved Suffering

Do not be surprised that you are sometimes unjustly accused. I Myself first drank this cup of undeserved suffering for love of you (*Diary*, 289).

1934, Holy Thursday. Jesus said to me, **I desire that you make an offering of yourself for sinners and especially for those souls who have lost hope in God's mercy** (*Diary*, 308).

My Prayer Response:

Jesus, by the merits of Your undeserved sufferings for us, help those who are unjustly accused and suffering without hope. Give them courage, Lord, to endure their sufferings out of love for You and souls.

O Blood and Water

I will daily repeat this act of self-oblation by pronouncing the following prayer which You Yourself have taught me, Jesus:

"O Blood and Water which gushed forth from the Heart of Jesus as a Fount of Mercy for us, I trust in You!" (*Diary*, 309).

I am giving you a share in the redemption of mankind. You are solace in My dying hour (*Diary*, 310).

My Prayer Response:

Jesus, You taught St. Faustina to daily renew her oblation of herself for sinners and so share in Your redemption of mankind by a prayer of trust: **O Blood and Water which gushed forth from the Heart of Jesus as a Fount of Mercy for us, I trust in You!** (*Diary*, 309). Help me to trust in You even more!

Love More Ardently

My will has not yet been fully accomplished in you; you will still remain on earth, but not for long. I am well pleased with your trust, but your love should be more ardent (*Diary,* 324).

My Prayer Response:

Lord Jesus, help me to trust in You more and to love You more ardently, so I may fulfill Your will. May Your will be fully accomplished in my life.

Thinking about Poor Sinners

Pure love gives the soul strength at the very moment of dying. When I was dying on the cross, I was not thinking about Myself, but about poor sinners, and I prayed for them to My Father (*Diary,* 324).

My Prayer Response:

Jesus, may Your pure love give me strength to love and pray for sinners. Have mercy on us all. And thank You, Lord, that on the cross, You were not thinking of Yourself but of us poor sinners.

In Union with Your Sufferings

I want your last moments to be completely similar to Mine on the cross. There is but one price at which souls are bought, and that is suffering united to My suffering on the cross. Pure love understands these words; carnal love will never understand them (*Diary*, 324)**.**

My Prayer Response:

Jesus, may Your love help me to offer my sufferings in union with Your sufferings on the cross for the salvation of souls. May my last moments be similar to Yours on the cross. All for the love of souls, Lord!

Just a Few More Drops

I have been waiting to share My suffering with you, for who can understand My suffering better than My spouse? (*Diary*, 348).

My child, just a few more drops in your chalice; it won't be long now (*Diary*, 694).

My Prayer Response:

Lord Jesus, help me to understand Your sufferings with my mind and heart. Help me not to waste the sufferings that I do have — but to offer them to You — because they are precious to You for the salvation of souls.

Victim Souls for Priests

My daughter, why are you weeping? After all, you yourself offered to undertake these sufferings. Know that what you have taken upon yourself for that soul is only a small portion. He [Father Sopocko] **is suffering much more** (*Diary*, 596).

My daughter, suffering will be a sign to you that I am with you (*Diary*, 669).

My Prayer Response:

Lord Jesus, as St. Faustina took on the sufferings of Father Michael Sopocko, her spiritual director and confessor, please accept the sufferings of victim souls offered for priests. And remind me, Lord, to offer my own sufferings for priests.

Part One:
A Whole-Burnt Offering

February 7, [1937]. Today, the Lord said to me, **I demand of you a perfect and whole-burnt offering; an offering of the will. No other sacrifice can compare with this one. I Myself am directing your life and arranging things in such a way that you will be for Me a continual sacrifice and will always do My will** (*Diary*, 923).

My Prayer Response:

Jesus, raise up many souls like St. Faustina to live a perfect and whole-burnt offering of their will to Your will. May they bring many souls to You!

Part Two: A Whole-Burnt Offering

And for the accomplishment of this offering, you will unite yourself with Me on the Cross. I know what you can do. I Myself will give you many orders directly, but I will delay the possibility of their being carried out and make it depend on others (*Diary*, 923).

My Prayer Response:

Lord Jesus, You know how weak I am. You know I want to do Your will, but I get detoured and distracted. In the words of St. Bernard, help me "to lean on You, my Beloved."

Part Three: A Whole-Burnt Offering

But what the superiors will not manage to do, I Myself will accomplish directly in your soul. And in the most hidden depths of your soul, a perfect holocaust will be carried out, not just for a while, but know, My daughter, that this offering will last until your death (*Diary*, 923).

My Prayer Response:

Thank You, Jesus, for the promise that You will do what I cannot do. May I live the total surrender to You that You promise to souls who desire to be a perfect holocaust for the salvation of souls.

Part Four: A Whole-Burnt Offering

But there is time, so that I the Lord will fulfill all your wishes. I delight in you as in a living host; let nothing terrify you; I am with you (*Diary*, 923).

My daughter, too great are your demands. "Jesus, You know that for You it is easier to grant much rather than a little." **That is so, it is less difficult for Me to grant a soul much rather than a little, but every conversion of a sinful soul demands sacrifice. … My dear daughter, I comply with your request** (*Diary*, 961).

My Prayer Response:

Lord Jesus, may I learn to pray like St. Faustina who made demands of You that are **too great** (*Diary*, 961). St. Faustina asked that You grant the grace of conversion to as many souls as the number of stitches that she made on a particular day with the crochet hook. She said that it is all she could do under holy obedience in her sickness: simple stitching. And the Lord complied with her request!

A Thirst for Souls

During Holy Mass, I saw the Lord Jesus nailed upon the cross amidst great torments. A soft moan issued from His Heart. After some time, He said, **I thirst. I thirst for the salvation of souls. Help Me, My daughter, to save souls. Join your sufferings to My Passion and offer them to the heavenly Father for sinners** (*Diary*, 1032).

My Prayer Response:

Lord Jesus, I hear Your cry of **I Thirst**. Help me to offer even the little sufferings I endure, as well as the big ones, for the salvation of souls. With Your help, I join them to Your Passion and offer them to the heavenly Father for sinners.

Lean on the Beloved

March 25, 1937. Holy Thursday. During Holy Mass, I saw the Lord, who said to me, **Lean your head on My breast and rest.** The Lord pressed me to His Heart and said, **I shall give you a small portion of My Passion, but do not be afraid, be brave; do not seek relief, but accept everything with submission to My will** (*Diary*, 1053).

My Prayer Response:

Lord Jesus, "I lean on You, my Beloved" (St. Bernard) for the rest and strength I need to accept everything with submission to Your will. Help me to be brave in sharing a small portion of Your Passion.

Refreshment for the Lord's Heart

Lie down and take your rest. I have let you experience in three hours what I suffered during the whole night (*Diary,* 1054).

My host, you are refreshment for My tormented Heart (*Diary,* 1056).

My Prayer Response:

Lord Jesus, thank You for the suffering You endured for me. May I be a refreshment for Your tormented Heart. And give me the strength to suffer out of love for You and others.

Contemplate My Wounds

In the evening, I saw the Lord Jesus upon the cross. From His hands, feet, and side the Most Sacred Blood was flowing. After some time, Jesus said to me, **All this is for the salvation of souls. Consider well, My daughter, what you are doing for their salvation.** I answered, "Jesus, when I look at Your suffering, I see that I am doing next to nothing for the salvation of souls." And the Lord said to me, **Know, My daughter, that your silent day-to-day martyrdom in complete submission to My will ushers many souls into heaven. And when it seems to you that your suffering exceeds your strength, contemplate My wounds, and you will rise above human scorn and judgment. Meditation on My Passion will help you rise above all things** (*Diary*, 1184).

My Prayer Response:

Inspire me, Lord Jesus, to consider what I can do for the salvation of souls. Teach me to contemplate the wounds of Your Passion and rise above human scorn and judgment.

Mercy in Spirit

Daughter, I need sacrifice lovingly accomplished, because that alone has meaning for Me. Enormous indeed are the debts of the world which are due to Me; pure souls can pay them by their sacrifice, exercising mercy in spirit (*Diary,* 1316).

My Prayer Response:

Jesus, teach me to lovingly make sacrifices for souls that I may exercise mercy in spirit. May I always remember that only what is accomplished in love has meaning for You, Lord.

An Instrument for the Conversion of Souls

Once, when I was passing by a group of people, I asked the Lord if they were all in the state of grace, because I did not feel His sufferings. **Because you do not feel My sufferings, it does not follow that they must all be in the state of grace. At times, I allow you to be aware of the condition of certain souls, and I give you the grace of suffering solely because I use you as the instrument of their conversion** (*Diary*, 1357).

My Prayer Response:

Lord, may I be sensitive to the conditions of certain souls, so I may exercise "mercy in spirit" for them. Through the inspiration of the Holy Spirit, help me to be an instrument of their conversion.

Suffering to Rescue Souls

My daughter, your struggle will last until death. Your last breath will mark its end. You shall conquer by meekness (*Diary*, 1597).

I have need of your sufferings to rescue souls (*Diary*, 1612).

My Prayer Response:

Jesus, help me not to waste my sufferings, little or great, because You need my sufferings to rescue souls. Keep me meek before You as I suffer and pray for souls.

The School of Suffering

The Lord said to me, **I am taking you into My school for the whole of Lent. I want to teach you how to suffer.** I answered, "With You, Lord, I am ready for everything." And I heard a voice, **You are allowed to drink from the cup from which I drink. I give you that exclusive privilege today ...** (*Diary*, 1626).

My Prayer Response:

Jesus, be my teacher on how to suffer, so I might teach others. I know that we all suffer, but so much of the suffering of the whole world is wasted! May I drink from the cup from which You drank, Lord.

Teaching on Feelings

During Holy Mass, I saw Jesus stretched out on the Cross, and He said to me, **My pupil, have great love for those who cause you suffering. Do good to those who hate you.** I answered, "O my Master, You see very well that I feel no love for them, and that troubles me." Jesus answered, **It is not always within your power to control your feelings. You will recognize that you have love if, after having experienced annoyance and contradiction, you do not lose your peace, but pray for those who have made you suffer and wish them well** (*Diary,* 1628).

My Prayer Response:

Thank You, Jesus, for teaching me about my feelings when annoyed by people. Help me to love them and remain in peace. Whenever I think of them, remind me to pray for them.

Mission of Mercy

My daughter, give Me souls. Know that it is your mission to win souls for Me by prayer and sacrifice, and by encouraging them to trust in My mercy (*Diary,* 1690).

My Prayer Response:

Lord Jesus, help me to win souls for You by prayer and sacrifice. Help me to encourage souls to trust in Your mercy. Like St. Faustina, the great Apostle of Divine Mercy, may I make this my mission in life.

When Sufferings Are Great

My daughter, know that if I allow you to feel and have a more profound knowledge of My sufferings, that is a grace from Me. But when your mind is dimmed and your sufferings are great, it is then that you take an active part in My Passion, and I am conforming you more fully to Myself. It is your task to submit yourself to My will at such times, more than at others ... (*Diary,* 1697).

My Prayer Response:

Lord Jesus, when things get tough and I get fatigued and my mind is dimmed and the sufferings are great — help me at such times to submit to Your will even more! At just such times, may I take an active part in Your Passion.

End Times and Eternal Life

November 21 – December 2

In this section, I placed the two themes of the "End Times" and "Eternal Life" under one introduction, because they are connected. The end times are a preparation for eternal life, and eternal life is the fulfillment of the promises of the Lord. In hope, we should look forward to what the Lord has prepared for us. We should desire it, ask for it, and give thanks. Recall what Jesus said in His Last Supper discourses in the Gospel of John: "In My Father's house there are many dwelling places. If there were not, would I have told you that I am going to prepare a place for you? And If I go and prepare a place for you, I will come back again and take you to Myself, so that where I am you also may be" (Jn 14:2-3).

The end times are the tough times of warning and chastisement to awaken mankind of the need to turn with trust to receive the Lord's mercy. Jesus told St. Faustina:

> **Write down these words, My daughter. Speak to the world about My mercy; let all mankind recognize My unfathomable mercy. It is a sign for the end times; after it will come the day of justice. While there is still time, let them have recourse to the fount of My mercy; let them profit from the Blood and Water which gushed forth for them** (*Diary*, 848).

The Lord's great desire is to show mercy to every soul

(see 1 Tim 2:4) and bring all humanity to eternal life. But it depends on our cooperation with His mercy. Our final destination depends on our desire and choice to surrender to God's will and His mercy.

In this vale of tears that we know as earthly life, surrendering to God's will and His mercy can be a challenge. We need to start anew every day. We can be encouraged by the Lord's words to St. Faustina about the reality of heaven, which awaits us:

> **When, in heaven, you see these present days, you will rejoice and will want to see as many of them as possible. I am not surprised, My daughter, that you cannot understand this now, because your heart is overflowing with pain and longing for Me. Your vigilance pleases Me. Let My word be enough for you, it will not be long now** (*Diary*, 1787).

May we take comfort in knowing that in God's time, it will not be long before He takes us home to be with Him forever. And may we claim the promise of eternal life even as we work out our salvation with fear and trembling.

King of Mercy

Write this: before I come as the Just Judge, I am coming first as the King of Mercy. Before the day of justice arrives, there will be given to people a sign in the heavens of this sort:

All light in the heavens will be extinguished, and there will be great darkness over the whole earth. Then the sign of the cross will be seen in the sky, and from the openings where the hands and the feet of the Savior were nailed will come forth great lights which will light up the earth for a period of time. This will take place shortly before the last day (*Diary,* 83).

My Prayer Response:

Lord Jesus, come now as the King of Mercy. We so need Your mercy, Lord. May the sign of Your cross draw all of mankind to Your merciful Love. May we desire Your mercy, ask for it, and receive it with thanksgiving.

The Lord's Final Coming

When, on one occasion, instead of interior prayer, I took up a book of spiritual reading, I heard these words spoken distinctly and forcefully within my soul, **You will prepare the world for My final coming.** These words moved me deeply, and although I pretended not to hear them, I understood them very well and had no doubt about them. Once, being tired out from this battle of love with God, and making constant excuses on the grounds that I was unable to carry out this task, I wanted to leave the chapel, but some force held me back and I found myself powerless. Then I heard these words, **You intend to leave the chapel, but you shall not get away from Me, for I am everywhere. You cannot do anything of yourself, but with Me you can do all things** (*Diary*, 429).

My Prayer Response:

Lord Jesus, without You, we can do nothing, but with You and Your gracious mercy, we can do all things (see Phil 4:13). Help us as apostles of Your Divine Mercy to prepare for and pray for Your final coming. May our celebration and offering of Holy Mass hasten the day of Your coming.

A Sign for the End Times

Write down these words, My daughter. Speak to the world about My mercy; let all mankind recognize My unfathomable mercy. It is a sign for the end times; after it will come the day of justice. While there is still time, let them have recourse to the fount of My mercy; let them profit from the Blood and Water which gushed forth for them.

O human souls, where are you going to hide on the day of God's anger: Take refuge now in the fount of God's mercy. O what a great multitude of souls I see! They worshiped The Divine Mercy and will be singing the hymn of praise for all eternity (*Diary*, 848).

My Prayer Response:

Lord Jesus, we pray with St. Faustina, Your great Apostle of Divine Mercy: Help us to take refuge *now* in the fount of Your Divine Mercy. Immerse us in the ocean of Your mercy, so even *now* we may "sing of the mercies of the Lord forever" (Ps 89:2).

The Door of Mercy

Today, I heard in my soul these words: **My daughter, it is time for you to take action; I am with you. Great persecutions and sufferings are in store for you, but be comforted by the thought that many souls will be saved and sanctified by this work** (*Diary,* 966).

Write: before I come as a just Judge, I first open wide the door of My mercy. He who refuses to pass through the door of My mercy must pass through the door of My justice … (*Diary,* 1146).

My Prayer Response:

Lord Jesus, may we be apostles of The Divine Mercy message and devotion with the help of St. Faustina. Help us to proclaim Your mercy, so many may pass through the door of Your mercy while it is open!

Be Always Ready

Today I said to the Lord, "When will You take me to Yourself. I've been feeling so ill, and I've been waiting for Your coming with such longing!" Jesus answered me, **Be always ready; I will not leave you in this exile for long. My holy will must be fulfilled in you.** O Lord, if Your holy will has not yet been entirely fulfilled in me, here I am, ready for everything that You want, O Lord! O my Jesus, there is only one thing which surprises me; namely, that You make so many secrets known to me; but that one secret — the hour of my death — You do not want to tell me. And the Lord answered me, **Be at peace; I will let you know, but not just now** (*Diary*, 1539).

My Prayer Response:

Lord Jesus, prepare me for my own personal end times. May I fulfill Your will in my life and be at peace with Your perfect timing for my death and entrance into eternal life with You.

True Knowledge of Self

I saw Jesus, and from His Heart there issued those same two rays, which enveloped me, whole and entire. At the same moment, all my torments vanished. **My daughter,** the Lord said, **know that of yourself you are just what you have gone through, and it is only by My grace that you are a participant of eternal life and all the gifts I lavish on you.** And with these words of the Lord, there came to me a true knowledge of myself. Jesus is giving me a lesson in deep humility and, at the same time, one of total trust in Him. My heart is reduced to dust and ashes, and even if all people were to trample me under their feet, I would still consider that a favor (*Diary*, 1559).

My Prayer Response:

Thank You, Lord Jesus, for the graces and mercy You have lavished on me. Without them, *I am nothing*, but with them and only with them, I am a participant of eternal life. May I live in this true knowledge of myself.

Day of Mercy

Today I heard the words: **In the Old Covenant I sent prophets wielding thunderbolts to My people. Today I am sending you with My mercy to the people of the whole world. I do not want to punish aching mankind, but I desire to heal it, pressing it to My Merciful Heart. I use punishment when they themselves force Me to do so; My hand is reluctant to take hold of the sword of justice. Before the Day of Justice I am sending the Day of Mercy.** I replied, "O my Jesus, speak to souls Yourself, because my words are insignificant" (*Diary*, 1588).

My Prayer Response:

Thank You, Jesus, for the "Day of Mercy" You announced to St. Faustina. As apostles of Divine Mercy, may we announce to the fearful people of the world Your mercy and Your desire to heal them and press them to Your Merciful Heart.

Part One: Convents and Churches

I will allow convents and churches to be destroyed. I answered, "Jesus, but there are so many souls praising You in convents." The Lord answered, **That praise wounds My Heart, because love has been banished from convents. Souls without love and without devotion, souls full of egoism and self-love, souls full of pride and arrogance, souls full of deceit and hypocrisy, lukewarm souls who have just enough warmth to keep them alive: My Heart cannot bear this. All the graces that I pour out upon them flow off them as off the face of a rock. I cannot stand them, because they are neither good or bad. I called convents into being to sanctify the world through them. It is from them that a powerful flame of love and sacrifice should burst forth** (*Diary*, 1702).

My Prayer Response:

Lord Jesus, in our day we see convents, rectories, and churches closed and destroyed. Help us to be enkindled by our first love! (see Rev 2:4).

Part Two: Convents and Churches

How can they sit on the promised throne of judgment to judge the world, when their guilt is greater than the guilt of the world? There is neither penance nor atonement. O heart, which received Me in the morning and at noon are all ablaze with hatred against Me, hatred of all sorts! O heart specially chosen by Me, were you chosen for this, to give Me more pain? (*Diary,* 1702).

When I tried to intercede for them, I could find nothing with which to excuse them and, being at the time unable to think of anything in their defense, my heart was seized with pain, and I wept bitterly. Then the Lord looked at me kindly and comforted me with these words: **Do not cry. There are still a great number of souls who love Me very much, but My Heart desires to be loved by all and, because My love is great, that is why I warn and chastise them** (*Diary,* 1703).

My Prayer Response:

Lord Jesus, raise up many faithful people who love You with a great fervor! Set many hearts on fire!

The Beauty of Heaven

I went across the garden one afternoon and stopped on the shore of the lake; I stood there for a long time, contemplating my surroundings. Suddenly, I saw the Lord Jesus near me, and He graciously said to me, **All this I created for you, My spouse; and know that all this beauty is nothing compared to what I have prepared for you in eternity** (*Diary*, 158).

"You know very well, O Jesus, that I am constantly swooning because of my longing for You." **Know this, My daughter, that you are already tasting now what other souls will obtain only in eternity** (*Diary*, 969).

My Prayer Response:

Lord Jesus, the sight of the beauty of Your creation stirs up within me a desire to see the beauty of heaven. "Draw me with Your love that I may be drawn" (Fr. Hauschert, SJ).

To the Full

When I received Holy Communion, I said to Him, "Jesus, I thought about You so many times last night," and Jesus answered me, **And I thought of you before I called you into being.** "Jesus, in what way were You thinking about me?" **In terms of admitting you to My eternal happiness.** After these words, my soul was flooded with the love of God. I could not stop marveling at how much God loves us (*Diary*, 1292).

On my way to the veranda, I went into the chapel for a moment. My heart was plunged in profound adoration, praising God's incomprehensible goodness and His mercy. Then I heard these words in my soul: **I am and will be for you such as you praise Me for being. You shall experience My goodness, already in this life and then, to the full, in the life to come** (*Diary*, 1707).

My Prayer Response:

Lord Jesus, may I think of You and praise and thank You more fervently and constantly in anticipation of what You have prepared in heaven for me and all those who love You!

This Vale of Tears

When I met with the Lord, I said to Him, "You are fooling me, Jesus; You show me the open gate of heaven, and again You leave me on earth." The Lord said to me, **When, in heaven, you see these present days, you will rejoice and will want to see as many of them as possible. I am not surprised, My daughter, that you cannot understand this now, because your heart is overflowing with pain and longing for Me. Your vigilance pleases Me. Let My word be enough for you; it will not be long now** (*Diary*, 1787).

My Prayer Response:

Lord Jesus, I long to see Your face and rejoice in Your presence as I live in this vale of tears. Give me courage, Lord, to persevere in serving You until You call me home to be with You forever.

Conversations with the Merciful Savior

December 3 – 23

These conversations of the Merciful Savior with various souls have already been published in a booklet as *Conversations with the Merciful God* (Marian Press, Stockbridge, MA 01263). Let me share some key insights about Jesus' conversations with such souls from the Preface and Introduction to the booklet.

In the Preface, I write:

> Don't we all wish we could talk to the Lord God and have some answers? We are all searching and in need of God's mercy in this "vale of tears."
>
> These conversations of the merciful God recorded by St. Faustina in the fifth notebook of her *Diary* are a summary of the message and devotion of the Merciful Savior. I purposely said devotion "of" the Merciful Savior because this is not just another devotion, but rather it is God's devotion to us!

Then in the Introduction, Vinny Flynn writes:

> In the fifth notebook of her *Diary,* Saint Faustina records conversations between the Merciful Savior and five souls. He speaks with a sinful soul, a despairing soul, a suffering soul, a soul striving after perfection, and a perfect soul.
>
> As we read, it becomes clear that these are not five different kinds of souls, but rather five

> conditions in which our souls may find themselves at particular times. We all tend to move in and out of these conditions, partially or completely, throughout our lives.
>
> On one level, these may be interpreted as actual conversations that Saint Faustina had with our Lord at various times during the ups and downs of her own spiritual journey. But the brief introduction she gives at the beginning of her *Diary* makes it clear that they also represent our Lord's merciful invitation to all of us to come to Him and experience His goodness and mercy present for us in the Eucharist.

Inspired by this last insight on the Lord's merciful invitation to each of us in these conversations, I have given you the opportunity to make your own response to the Lord, with the exception of the first response given by St. Faustina for the despairing soul. May this opportunity to respond draw you into deeper intimacy with the Merciful Savior.

Part One: With a Sinful Soul

The Goodness of God.

The mercy of God, hidden in the Blessed Sacrament, the voice of the Lord who speaks to us from the throne of mercy: **Come to Me, all of you.**

Conversation of the Merciful God with a Sinful Soul.

Jesus: **Be not afraid of your Savior, O sinful soul. I make the first move to come to you, for I know that by yourself you are unable to lift yourself to Me. Child, do not run away from your Father; be willing to talk openly with your God of mercy who wants to speak words of pardon and lavish His graces on you. How dear your soul is to Me! I have inscribed your name upon My hand; you are engraved as a deep wound in My Heart** (*Diary,* 1485).

Soul: Your response.

My Prayer Response:

Lord Jesus, reach out to us sinful souls. Take the first steps toward us. In our need and shame, we are afraid to approach You. So, please draw us with compassionate mercy to Your loving Heart.

Part Two: With a Sinful Soul

Jesus: **I am your strength, I will help you in the struggle.**

Soul: Your response.

Jesus: **My child, do you fear the God of mercy? My holiness does not prevent Me from being merciful. Behold, for you I have established a throne of mercy on earth — the tabernacle — and from this throne I desire to enter into your heart. I am not surrounded by a retinue or guards. You can come to Me at any moment, at any time; I want to speak to you and desire to grant you grace** (*Diary,* 1485).

Soul: Your response.

My Prayer Response:

Lord, before the throne of mercy on earth, the tabernacle of Your Eucharistic Presence, I ask for mercy for souls that are afraid of You. Be especially merciful to them and draw them to Yourself.

Part Three: With a Sinful Soul

Jesus: **My mercy is greater than your sins and those of the entire world. Who can measure the extent of My goodness? For you I descended from heaven to earth; for you I allowed Myself to be nailed to the cross; for you I let My Sacred Heart be pierced with a lance, thus opening wide the source of mercy for you. Come, then, with trust to draw graces from this fountain. I never reject a contrite heart. Your misery has disappeared in the depths of My mercy. Do not argue with Me about your wretchedness. You will give Me pleasure if you hand over to Me all your troubles and griefs. I shall heap upon you the treasures of My grace** (*Diary*, 1485).

Soul: Your response.

My Prayer Response:

Lord Jesus, reveal to souls that Your mercy is greater than all the sins of the world. Draw us to Your Sacred Heart, so our miseries may disappear in the depths of Your mercy. Have mercy on us all.

Part Four: With a Sinful Soul

Jesus: **Child, speak no more of your misery; it is already forgotten. Listen, My child, to what I desire to tell you. Come close to My wounds and draw from the Fountain of Life whatever your heart desires. Drink copiously from the Fountain of Life and you will not weary on your journey. Look at the splendor of My mercy and do not fear the enemies of your salvation. Glorify My mercy** (*Diary,* 1485).

Soul: Your response.

My Prayer Response:

Lord Jesus, I draw close to You in the Blessed Sacrament and drink from the Fountain of Life for strength on my journey. I glorify Your mercy.

Part One: With a Despairing Soul

Jesus: **O soul steeped in darkness, … . Come and confide in your God, who is love and mercy.**

— But the soul, deaf even to this appeal, wraps itself in darkness.

Jesus calls out again: **My child, listen to the voice of your merciful Father.**

— In the soul arises this reply: "For me there is no mercy," and it falls into greater darkness … .

Jesus calls to the soul a third time, but the soul remains deaf and blind, hardened and despairing. Then the mercy of God begins to exert itself, and, without any co-operation from the soul, God grants it final grace. … The soul knows that this, for her, is final grace and, should it show even a flicker of good will, the mercy of God will accomplish the rest.

My omnipotent mercy is active here. Happy the soul that takes advantage of this grace (*Diary,* 1486).

My Prayer Response:

Lord Jesus, Your all-powerful mercy is active in the despairing soul. Continue to give it graces.

Part Two: With a Despairing Soul

Jesus: **What joy fills My Heart when you return to Me. Because you are weak, I take you in My arms and carry you to the home of My Father.**

Soul (as if awakening, asks fearfully): Your response.

Jesus: **... My child. You have a special claim on My mercy. Let it act in your poor soul; let the rays of grace enter your soul; they bring with them light, warmth, and life** (*Diary,* 1486).

Soul: Your response.

My Prayer Response:

Lord Jesus, shine Your rays of warmth and life into the darkness of souls who are despairing. Claim such souls by the grace of Your mercy. And keep me, Lord, from ever despairing of Your mercy.

Part Three: With a Despairing Soul

Jesus: **My child, all your sins have not wounded My Heart as painfully as your present lack of trust does — that after so many efforts of My love and mercy, you should still doubt My goodness.**

Soul: Your response.

Jesus: **Here, soul, are all the treasures of My Heart. Take everything you need from it** (*Diary,* 1486).

Soul: Your response.

My Prayer Response:

Lord Jesus, draw souls in despair to trust in You and not to doubt Your goodness. Share with them all the treasures of Your Heart.

Part Four: With a Despairing Soul

Jesus: **Tell Me all, My child, hide nothing from Me, because My loving Heart, the Heart of your Best Friend, is listening to you.**

Soul: Your response.

Jesus (interrupting): **Do not be absorbed in your misery — you are still too weak to speak of it — but, rather, gaze on My Heart filled with goodness, and be imbued with My sentiments. Strive for meekness and humility; be merciful to others, as I am to you; and, when you feel your strength failing, if you come to the fountain of mercy to fortify your soul, you will not grow weary on your journey** (*Diary*, 1486).

Soul: Your response.

My Prayer Response:

Lord Jesus, draw souls overwhelmed by their miseries to gaze at Your Heart filled with goodness. Draw them to the fountain of mercy to strengthen them on their journey. Teach them to be meek and humble. And teach them to be merciful as You are to them.

Part One: With a Suffering Soul

Jesus: **Poor soul, I see that you suffer much and that you do not have even the strength to converse with Me. So I will speak to you. Even though your sufferings were very great, do not lose heart or give in to despondency. But tell Me, My child, who has dared to wound your heart? Tell Me about everything, be sincere in dealing with Me, reveal all the wounds of your heart. I will heal them, and your suffering will become a source of your sanctification** (*Diary,* 1487).

Soul: Your response.

My Prayer Response:

Lord Jesus, in my suffering I reveal the wounds of my heart, so You may heal them. May my suffering become a source of my sanctification.

Part Two: With a Suffering Soul

Jesus: **My child, do not be discouraged. I know your boundless trust in Me; I know you are aware of My goodness and mercy. Let us talk in detail about everything that weighs so heavily upon your heart.**

Soul: Your response.

Jesus: **Talk to Me simply, as a friend to a friend. Tell Me now, My child, what hinders you from advancing in holiness?** (*Diary*, 1487).

Soul: Your response.

My Prayer Response:

Lord Jesus, please help me to talk to You freely about things that weigh upon my heart. And also help me to listen to You as You direct me in my response to these painful situations.

Part Three: With a Suffering Soul

Jesus: **True, My child, all that is painful. But there is no way to heaven except the way of the cross. I followed it first. You must learn that it is the shortest and surest way.**

Soul: Your response.

Jesus: **It is because you are not of this world that the world hates you. First it persecuted Me. Persecution is a sign that you are following in My footsteps faithfully** (*Diary*, 1487).

Soul: Your response.

My Prayer Response:

Lord Jesus, help me to learn with my heart what I know with my head, that the cross is the only, shortest, and surest way to heaven. You led the way first. Give me the strength to follow.

Part Four: With a Suffering Soul

Jesus: **Well, My child, this time you have told Me a good deal. I realize how painful it is not to be understood, and especially by those whom one loves and with whom one has been very open. But suffice it to know that I understand all your troubles and misery. I am pleased by the deep faith you have, despite everything, in My representatives. Learn from this that no one will understand a soul entirely — that is beyond human ability. Therefore, I have remained on earth to comfort your aching heart and to fortify your soul, so that you will not falter on the way. You say that a dense darkness is obscuring your mind. But why, at such times, do you not come to Me, the light who can in an instant pour into your soul more understanding about holiness than can be found in any books?** (*Diary,* 1487).

Soul: Your response.

My Prayer Response:

Thank You, Jesus, for understanding all my troubles and miseries. Help me to come to You for light and comfort that only You can give me.

Part Five: With a Suffering Soul

Jesus: **Know, too, that the darkness about which you complain I first endured in the Garden of Olives when My Soul was crushed in mortal anguish. I am giving you a share in those sufferings because of My special love for you and in view of the high degree of holiness I am intending for you in heaven. A suffering soul is closest to My Heart** (*Diary*, 1487).

Soul: Your response.

My Prayer Response:

Lord Jesus, thank You for suffering out of love for me. Thank You for giving me a share in Your suffering in view of what You have prepared for me in heaven.

Part Six: With a Suffering Soul

Jesus: **My child, make the resolution never to rely on people. Entrust yourself completely to My will saying, "Not as I want, but according to Your will, O God, let it be done unto me." These words, spoken from the depths of one's heart, can raise a soul to the summit of sanctity in a short time. In such a soul I delight. Such a soul gives Me glory. Such a soul fills heaven with the fragrance of her virtue. But understand that the strength by which you bear sufferings comes from frequent Communions. So approach this fountain of mercy often, to draw with the vessel of trust whatever you need** (*Diary,* 1487).

Soul: Your response.

My Prayer Response:

Lord Jesus, I entrust myself completely to You. "Not my will, but Yours be done unto me." May I draw strength to bear the cross You offer me by drawing strength from Holy Communion, both Sacramental and Spiritual Communions.

Part One: With a Soul Striving after Perfection

Jesus: **I am pleased with your efforts, O soul aspiring for perfection, but why do I see you so often sad and depressed? Tell Me, My child, what is the meaning of this sadness, and what is its cause?**

Soul: Your response.

Jesus: **You see, My child, what you are of yourself. The cause of your falls is that you rely too much upon yourself and too little on Me. But let this not sadden you so much. You are dealing with the God of mercy, which your misery cannot exhaust. Remember, I did not allot only a certain number of pardons** (*Diary,* 1488).

Soul: Your response.

My Prayer Response:

Lord Jesus, You know my miseries better than I do. I want to do better. I want to rely more on You. Help me to plunge into the ocean of Your mercies, so my miseries may be transformed into a plea for mercy on the whole world.

Part Two: With a Soul Striving after Perfection

Jesus: **My child, know that the greatest obstacles to holiness are discouragement and an exaggerated anxiety. These will deprive you of the ability to practice virtue. All temptations united together ought not disturb your interior peace, not even momentarily. Sensitiveness and discouragement are the fruits of self-love. You should not become discouraged, but strive to make My love reign in place of your self-love. Have confidence, My child. Do not lose heart in coming for pardon, for I am always ready to forgive you. As often as you beg for it, you glorify My mercy** (*Diary*, 1488).

Soul: Your response.

My Prayer Response:

Lord Jesus, You certainly put Your finger on my problem — exaggerated anxiety. Help me to make Your love reign in place of my self-love. Help me with Your mercy.

Part Three: With a Soul Striving after Perfection

Jesus: **My child, life on earth is a struggle indeed; a great struggle for My kingdom. But fear not, because you are not alone. I am always supporting you, so lean on Me as you struggle, fearing nothing. Take the vessel of trust and draw from the fountain of life — for yourself, but also for other souls, especially such as are distrustful of My goodness** (*Diary*, 1488).

Soul: Your response.

My Prayer Response:

Lord Jesus, I take the vessel of trust and draw from the fountain of life. Help me to trust You even more! Help all souls striving for perfection to increase their capacity to trust in You.

Part One: With a Perfect Soul

Soul: My Lord and Master, I desire to converse with You.

Jesus: **Speak, My beloved child, for I am always listening. I wait for you. What do you desire to say?**

Soul: Your response.

Jesus: **Your words please Me, and your thanksgiving opens up new treasures of graces. But, My child, we should talk in more detail about the things that lie in your heart. Let us talk confidentially and frankly, as two hearts that love one another do** (*Diary*, 1489).

Soul: Your response

My Prayer Response:

My Lord Jesus, I want to love You more. I want to be faithful to Your will. I want to desire and long for You. I want to live the exhortation of St. Paul: "Rejoice always, Pray without ceasing, in all things give thanks, for this is the will of God in Christ Jesus regarding you all" (1 Thess 5:16-18).

Part Two: With a Perfect Soul

Jesus: **My beloved child, delight of My Heart, your words are dearer and more pleasing to Me than the angelic chorus. All the treasures of My Heart are open to you. Take from this Heart all that you need for yourself and for the whole world. For the sake of your love, I withhold the just chastisements, which mankind has deserved. A single act of pure love pleases Me more than a thousand imperfect prayers. One of your sighs of love atones for many offenses with which the godless overwhelm Me** (*Diary*, 1489).

Soul: Your response.

My Prayer Response:

My Lord Jesus, thank You for opening Your Heart with all its treasures. I take all I need for myself and for the whole world. What a loving God You are! The Church and the whole world need a sovereign act of Your mercy *now!*

Part Three: With a Perfect Soul

Jesus: **The smallest act of virtue has unlimited value in My eyes because of your great love for Me. In a soul that lives on My love alone, I reign as in heaven. I watch over it day and night. In it I find My happiness; My ear is attentive to each request of its heart; often I anticipate its requests. O child, especially beloved by Me, apple of My eye, rest a moment near My Heart and taste of the love in which you will delight for all eternity** (*Diary,* 1489).

Soul: Your response.

My Prayer Response:

My Lord Jesus, may I do everything out of love for You, even the smallest act. May I know Your love throughout eternity. I rest near Your Heart, Lord.

Part Four: With a Perfect Soul

Jesus: **But child, you are not yet in your homeland; so go, fortified by My grace, and fight for My kingdom in human souls; fight as a king's child would; and remember that the days of your exile will pass quickly, and with them the possibility of earning merit for heaven. I expect from you, My child, a great number of souls who will glorify My mercy for all eternity. My child, that you may answer My call worthily, receive Me daily in Holy Communion. It will give you strength ...** (*Diary*, 1489).

Soul: Your response.

My Prayer Response:

My Lord Jesus, strengthen me with Yourself in Holy Communion to proclaim Your merciful love, so many souls will glorify Your mercy for all eternity.

Humble Simplicity

December 24 – 31

As we enter into the joy and wonder of the Christmas season, the little Lord Jesus invites us to come to Him simply and humbly like children. So, to help you celebrate the season, we conclude *Divine Mercy Minutes with Jesus* with this section on the theme "Humble Simplicity."

The Lord Jesus teaches St. Faustina about humility and often uses the simplicity of a child as an example. He even appears to her as a child to strengthen His teaching, pointing to Himself as the supreme model of humble simplicity. Consider this appearance of a child to St. Faustina, who reveals to her that He Himself is the Lord God:

> A moment later, I again saw the child who had awakened me. It was of wondrous beauty and repeated these words to me, **True greatness of the soul is in loving God and in humility.** I asked the child, "How do you know that true greatness of the soul is in loving God and in humility? Only theologians know about such things and you haven't even learned your catechism. So how do you know?" To this He answered, **I know; I know all things.** And with that, He disappeared (*Diary*, 427).

Because humble simplicity is so important to our spiritual life, Jesus continued to appear to St. Faustina as a little child, keeping her company and forming her heart. This revelation to St. Faustina is a living example of the teaching of Jesus in Sacred Scripture: "Unless you turn and become like children, you will not enter the kingdom of heaven" (Mt 18:3).

May we ask the little Lord Jesus to make us humble and simple, especially as we celebrate His holy birth. As He works in our hearts, may we hear Him say to us — as He did to St. Faustina:

> **You are my great joy; your love and your humility make Me leave the heavenly throne and unite Myself with you. Love fills up the abyss between My greatness and your nothingness** (*Diary*, 512).

A Childlike Spirit

Holy Hour. During this hour, I tried to meditate on the Lord's Passion. But my soul was filled with joy, and suddenly I saw the Child Jesus. But His majesty penetrated me to such an extent that I said, "Jesus, You are so little, and yet I know that You are my Creator and Lord." And Jesus answered me, **I am, and I keep company with you as a child to teach you humility and simplicity** (*Diary*, 184).

Thursday. When I started the Holy Hour, I wanted to immerse myself in the agony of Jesus in the Garden of Olives. Then I heard a voice in my soul: **Meditate on the mystery of the Incarnation.** And suddenly the Infant Jesus appeared before me, radiant with beauty. He told me how much God is pleased with simplicity in a soul. **Although My greatness is beyond understanding, I commune only with those who are little. I demand of you a childlike spirit** (*Diary*, 332).

My Prayer Response:

Lord Jesus, teach me humility and simplicity. May I be childlike in my willingness and openness to learn. May I have a childlike spirit to grasp Your greatness.

True Greatness

In the evening, I just about got into bed, and I fell asleep immediately. Though I fell asleep quickly, I was awakened even more quickly. A little child came and woke me up. The child seemed about a year old, and I was surprised it could speak so well, as children of that age either do not speak or speak very indistinctly. The child was beautiful beyond words and resembled the Child Jesus, and he said to me, **Look at the sky.** And when I looked at the sky I saw the stars and the moon shining. Then the child asked me, **Do you see this moon and these stars?** When I said yes, he spoke these words to me, **These stars are the souls of faithful Christians, and the moon is the souls of religious. Do you see how great the difference is between the light of the moon and the light of the stars? Such is the difference in heaven between the soul of a religious and the soul of a faithful Christian.** And he went on to say that, **True greatness is in loving God and in humility** (*Diary*, 424).

My Prayer Response:

Lord Jesus, may I learn that true greatness is in loving You and in humility. May I learn to come to You as a child.

Again, the Lesson of Humility

A moment later, I again saw the child who had awakened me. It was of wondrous beauty and repeated these words to me, **True greatness of the soul is in loving God and in humility.** I asked the child, "How do you know that true greatness of the soul is in loving God and in humility? Only theologians know about such things and you haven't even learned the catechism. So how do you know?" To this He answered, **I know; I know all things.** And with that, He disappeared (*Diary,* 427).

The day of the renewal of vows. The presence of God flooded my soul. During Holy Mass I saw Jesus, and He said to me, **You are My great joy; your love and your humility make Me leave the heavenly throne and unite Myself with you. Love fills up the abyss that exists between My greatness and your nothingness** (*Diary,* 512).

My Prayer Response:

Lord, again You appeared as a child to St. Faustina and repeated Your teaching: **True greatness of the soul is in loving God and in humility.** Lord, make me humble.

Telling Jesus Everything

Today, the Lord said to me, **My daughter, I am told that there is much simplicity in you, so why do you not tell Me about everything that concerns you, even the smallest details? Tell Me about everything, and know that this will give Me great joy.** I answered, "But You know about everything, Lord." And Jesus replied to me, **Yes, I do know; but you should not excuse yourself with the fact that I know, but with childlike simplicity talk to Me about everything, for My ears and heart are inclined towards you, and your words are dear to Me** (*Diary,* 921).

My Prayer Response:

Lord Jesus, in childlike simplicity, help me talk with You about everything, because You delight in our conversing with You and in our trust in You.

Cuddling Close to Jesus' Heart

Today I heard these words: **My daughter, be always like a little child towards those who represent Me, otherwise you will not benefit from the graces I bestow on you through them** (*Diary,* 1260).

Today during Holy Mass, I saw the Infant Jesus near my kneeler. He appeared to be about one year old, and He asked me to take Him in my arms. When I did take Him in my arms, He cuddled up close to my bosom and said, **It is good for Me to be close to your heart.** "Although You are so little, I know that You are God. Why do You take the appearance of such a little baby to commune with me?" **Because I want to teach you spiritual childhood. I want you to be very little, because when you are little, I carry you close to My Heart, just as you are holding Me close to your heart right now** (*Diary,* 1481).

My Prayer Response:

Lord Jesus, You delight in our cuddling close to Your Heart, so You can teach us spiritual childhood. Thank You for the example of St. Faustina.

Simplicity Is More Pleasing ...

I saw myself in some kind of a palace; and Jesus gave me His hand, sat me at His side, and said with kindness, **My bride, you always please Me by your humility. The greatest misery does not stop Me from uniting Myself to a soul, but where there is pride, I am not there** (*Diary*, 1563).

February 27, [1938]. Today, I went to confession to Father An. [Andrasz] I did as Jesus wanted. After confession, a surge of light filled my soul. Then I heard a voice: **Because you are a child, you shall remain close to My Heart. Your simplicity is more pleasing to Me than your mortifications** (*Diary*, 1617).

My Prayer Response:

Lord Jesus, thank You for Your teaching to St. Faustina that You are always pleased by humility and that simplicity is more pleasing to You than mortifications.

Purity of Intention

When I was apologizing to the Lord Jesus for a certain action of mine which, a little later, turned out to be imperfect, Jesus put me at ease with these words: **My daughter, I reward you for the purity of your intention which you had at the time when you acted. My Heart rejoiced that you had My love under consideration at the time you acted, and that in so distinct a way; and even now you still derive benefit from this; that is, from the humiliation. Yes, My child, I want you to always have such great purity of intention in the very least things you undertake** (*Diary,* 1566).

My Prayer Response:

Thank You, Lord Jesus, for the lesson You taught St. Faustina about the purity of intention for our actions that delight You even if what we do is not perfect. Purify my heart, O Lord.

A Summary

Conclusion of the Retreat.

Last Conversation with the Lord.

Thank you, Eternal Love, for Your inconceivable kindness to me, that You would occupy Yourself directly with my sanctification. — **My daughter, let three virtues adorn you in a particular way: humility, purity of intention, and love. Do nothing beyond what I demand of you, and accept everything that My hand gives you. Strive for a life of recollection so that you can hear My voice, which is so soft that only recollected souls can hear it …** (*Diary,* 1779).

My Prayer Response:

Thank You, Lord, for summarizing Your teaching on sanctification that we should practice three special virtues: humility, purity of intention, and love. Help us to be recollected, so we can always hear Your voice teaching us. Bless us, Lord, in the New Year. Help us put this teaching into practice.

Thematic Index

B

C

D

E

F

G

H

I

J

L

M

N

P

S

T

U

W

Footnotes to the Novena Before the Feast of Mercy

See

Day 2 [1] In the original text, St. Faustina uses the pronoun "us" since she was offering this prayer as a consecrated religious sister. The wording adapted here is intended to make the prayer suitable for universal use.

Day 4 [2] Our Lord's original words here were "the pagans." Since the pontificate of Blessed Pope John XXIII, the Church has seen fit to replace this term with clearer and more appropriate terminology.

Day 5 [3] Our Lord's original words here were "heretics and schismatics," since He spoke to St. Faustina within the context of her times. As of the Second Vatican Council, Church authorities have seen fit not to use those designations in accordance with the explanation given in the Council's Decree on Ecumenism (n.3). Every Pope since the Council has reaffirmed that usage. Saint

Faustina herself, her heart always in harmony with the mind of the Church, most certainly would have agreed. When at one time, because of the decisions of her superiors and Father confessor, she was not able to execute our Lord's inspirations and orders, she declared: "I will follow Your will insofar as You will permit me to do so through Your representative. O my Jesus, I give priority to the voice of the Church over the voice with which You speak to me" (*Diary*, 497). The Lord confirmed her action and praised her for it.

Day 7 [4] The text leads one to conclude that in this prayer directed to Jesus, who is the Redeemer, it is "victim" souls and contemplatives that are being prayed for; those persons, that is, who voluntarily offered themselves to God for the salvation of their neighbor (see Col 1:24; 2 Cor 4:12). This explains their close union with the Savior and the extraordinary efficacy that their invisible activity has for others.

Day 9 [5] To understand who are the souls designated for this day, and who in the *Diary* are called "lukewarm," but are also compared to ice and to corpses, we would do well to take note of the definition that the Savior Himself gave to them when speaking to St. Faustina about them on one occasion: **There are souls who thwart My efforts**

(1682). **Souls without love or devotion, souls full of egoism and selfishness, proud and arrogant souls full of deceit and hypocrisy, lukewarm souls who have just enough warmth to keep themselves alive: My Heart cannot bear this. All the graces that I pour out upon them flow off them as off the face of a rock. I cannot stand them because they are neither good nor bad** (1702).

My Favorite Minutes with Jesus

My Favorite Minutes with Jesus

My Favorite Minutes with Jesus

Promoting Divine Mercy since 1941

Marian Press, the publishing apostolate of the Marian Fathers of the Immaculate Conception of the B.V.M., has published and distributed millions of religious books, magazines, and pamphlets that teach, encourage, and edify Catholics around the world. Our publications promote and support the ministry and spirituality of the Marians worldwide. Loyal to the Holy Father and to the teachings of the Catholic Church, the Marians fulfill their special mission by:

- Fostering devotion to Mary, the Immaculate Conception.
- Promoting The Divine Mercy message and devotion.
- Offering assistance to the dying and the deceased, especially the victims of war and disease.
- Promoting Christian knowledge, administering parishes, shrines, and conducting missions.

Based in Stockbridge, Mass., Marian Press is known as the publisher of the *Diary of Saint Maria Faustina Kowalska*, and the Marians are the leading authorities on The Divine Mercy message and devotion.

Stockbridge is also the home of the National Shrine of The Divine Mercy, the Association of Marian Helpers, and a destination for thousands of pilgrims each year.

Globally, the Marians' ministries also include missions in developing countries where the spiritual and material needs are enormous.

To learn more about the Marians, their spirituality, publications or ministries, visit **marian.org** or **thedivinemercy.org**, the Marians' website that is devoted exclusively to Divine Mercy.

New Releases from Marian Press

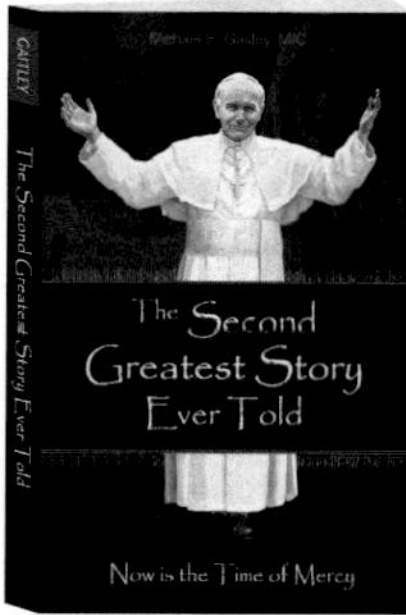

SGSBK 9781596143166

From the Bestselling Author of *33 Days to Morning Glory* and *Consoling the Heart of Jesus*

The Second Greatest Story Ever Told

In *The Second Greatest Story Ever Told* best-selling author Fr. Michael Gaitley, MIC, reveals St. John Paul II's witness for our time. Building on the prophetic voices of Margaret Mary Alacoque, Thérèse of Lisieux, Maximilian Kolbe, and Faustina Kowalska, *The Second Greatest Story Ever Told* is more than a historical account of the Great Mercy Pope. This book expounds on the profound connection between Divine Mercy and Marian consecration. It serves as an inspiration for all those who desire to bear witness to the mercy of God, focused on Christ and formed by Mary. Now is the time of mercy. Now is the time to make John Paul's story your own.

Faustina: The Mystic and Her Message

Follow the path of Faustina on her journey to sainthood. Award-winning author and historian Dr. Ewa Czaczkowska tenaciously pursued Faustina to ultimately produce a biography that masterfully tracks this mystic's riveting life and her unique call from Jesus. More than 70,000 copies of the original Polish edition were sold within three months of its release. Now licensed for English distribution exclusively through Marian Press, *Faustina: The Mystic and Her Message* provides new details about this remarkable woman and rare photographs of her. In this biography, get to know the real Faustina, her message, and her mission. 456 pages, 32-page photo insert, 7 x 9.5 inches.

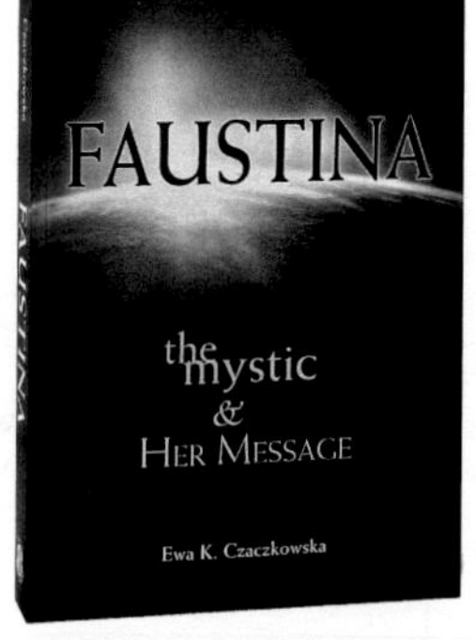

BIOSF 9781596143104

Divine Mercy Resources

Divine Mercy Explained and Divine Mercy Image Explained

Fr. Michael E. Gaitley, MIC

DMIX 9781596142770 ebook: EBDMIX

DMX 9781596142725 ebook: EBDMX

Start with *Divine Mercy Explained*, an easy-to-read, informative overview and introduction to the Divine Mercy message and devotion. Then, enjoy *The Divine Mercy Image Explained*, an engaging read that reveals hidden gems and highlights inspiring truths about the Divine Mercy Image. Together, these two engaging booklets bring depth and clarity to the message and devotion, especially the image.

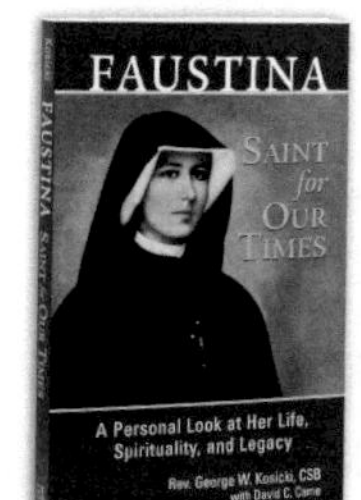

Faustina, Saint for Our Times

Fr. George W. Kosicki, CSB

SFT 9781596142268

Loved, Lost, Found: 17 Divine Mercy Conversions

Written by Felix Carroll, *Loved, Lost, Found* profiles 17 everyday people who discover God's extraordinary mercy. They include a former abortionist, a blind atheist, an unfaithful husband, and more. Soft cover, 6"x 9".

LLF16 9781596142749 ebook: EBLLF